Developing Skills

READING

for KS3 tests

Andrew Bennett • Clare Constant

Heinemann Educational Publishers
Halley Court, Jordan Hill, Oxford OX2 8EJ
Part of Harcourt Education

Heinemann is the registered trademark of Harcourt Education Limited

© Clare Constant and Andrew Bennett, 2003

First published 2003

07 06 05 04 03
10 9 8 7 6 5 4 3 2 1

British Library Cataloguing in Publication Data is available from the British Library on request.

ISBN 0 435 10640 6

Copyright notice
All rights reserved. No part of this publication may be reproduced in any form or by any means (including photocopying or storing it in any medium by electronic means and whether or not transiently or incidentally to some other use of this publication) without the written permission of the copyright owner, except in accordance with the provisions of the Copyright, Designs and Patents Act 1988 or under the terms of a licence issued by the Copyright Licensing Agency, 90 Tottenham Court Road, London W1T 4LP. Applications for the copyright owner's written permission should be addressed to the publisher.

Designed by Hicksdesign
Produced by Bridge Creative Services Limited, Bicester, Oxon
Original illustrations © Harcourt Education Limited, 2003
Illustrated by p9 Rhiannon Powell, p17, p20 Lisa Smith, p25, p67, p68, p127, p128 John Storey, p21, p30, Phil Healey, p31 Paul McCaffrey, p41 Jennifer Ward, p43, p99 Jackie Harland, p44-45, p46, p145 Alice Englander, p53 Georgian McBain, p89 Martin Fish, p93, p94 Beccy Blake, p107 Gary Wing, p114 Catherine Howes, p132 Georgina McBain

Cover photo © Photodisc
Cover design by GD Associates

Printed and bound in the UK by Bath Colourbooks

Acknowledgements
The publishers gratefully acknowledge the following for permission to reproduce copyright material.
Every effort has been made to contact copyright holders of material reproduced in this book.
Any omissions will be rectified in subsequent printings if notice is given to the publishers.

pp10–11 RSPCA and Jess Coppell for the battery hen advert; p15 Focus/Origin Publishing for 'Small world, isn't it?' from FOCUS, June 2002. Subscriptions tel: 01858 438822; p24 Express Newspapers for 'The man who left his mark on history – and the world's streets' by Jay Iliff, the Express, Wednesday 14th January 1998. © Express Newspapers; p26 Atlantic Syndication for 'The Weekly Menus' from the Daily Mail, 31st May 2002; p28 Allen & Unwin, Australia, for an extract from Remote Man by Elizabeth Honey. Copyright © Elizabeth Honey 2000. www.allen-unwin.com.au; p35 National Canine Defence League for an extract from their leaflet, 'Can we count on you?'. www.ncdl.org.uk; p45 Orion Publishing Group Limited for an extract from Don't Open Your Eyes by Ann Halam, published by Orion Children's Books; p46 Andersen Press Limited, for an extract from Ghost Behind The Wall by Melvin Burgess; p50 Atlantic Syndication for an extract from 'Bridget Jones Goes to the Pole' by Catherine Hartley, the Daily Mail, 23rd November 2002; p53 Faber and Faber Limited, for the use of 'Snowball' by Carol Ann Duffy, from Meeting Midnight; p58 Martin Bell for the use of 'Freeride>>Cliff Jump' by Martin Bell, published in Daily Mail Ski & Snowboard, September 2002. Copyright © Martin Bell; p63 Xbox Gamer magazine, for an extract from the article 'Amped: Freestyle Snowboarding' by Lee Hall, Xbox Gamer, March 2002; Microsoft Corporation for two screenshots from the game 'Amped: Freestyle Snowboarding', used with Xbox Gamer article; p68 Bloomsbury Publishing Plc for the use of an extract from Face by Benjamin Zephaniah; pp73–74 Ethiopiaid for an extract from one of their letters; p79 BBC News Online, Stephanie Wienrich and Steve Pankhurst for 'Charity calls for net-free day', found at http://newsbbc.co.uk/; p84 Hodder & Stoughton Limited for an extract from Secret Heart by David Almond; p89 Curtis Brown, London, on behalf of the Estate of Gerald Durrell, for an extract from Golden Bats and Pink Pigeons by Gerald Durrell. Copyright © Gerald Durrell 1977; p94 David Attenborough Productions Limited for the use of an extract from Life of Birds by David Attenborough, published by BBC Books 1998; p99 Hodder & Stoughton Limited for an extract from Sons of War by Melvyn Bragg; p104 Mrs R. B. H. Worthington for the use of 'Boxing – blows below the collar only' by the Reverend John Worthington, found at www.gloabalideasbank.org; p109 Edwin 'Flip' Homansky, MD for 'The Ultimate Question: Spit or Swallow?' found at www.secondsout.com; p118 Kazuo Tamayama and John Nunneley for an extract from Tales by Japanese Soldiers by Kazuo Tamayama and John Nunneley, published by Cassells in 2000; p123 Express Newspapers for 'How a Mum's Army patrol bought safety to the city where fear stalked streets' by Mark Lister, Sunday Express, 5th May 2002. Copyright © Express Newspapers; pp132–133 The Society of Authors, on behalf of the Bernard Shaw Estate, for an extract from Pygmalion by George Bernard Shaw; pp137–138 Professor Steve Jones for 'View from the lab: let's face it the eye can play strange tricks', 23rd April 1998, www.telegraph.co.uk; p144 HarperCollins Publishers for an extract from Addicted by Tony Adams; p145 The Penguin Group UK for an extract from The Go-Between by L. P. Hartley, (Hamish Hamilton, 1953) Copyright © 1953 by L. P. Hartley. This edition copyright © Douglas Brook-Douglas, 1997; p146 Macmillan Publishing for an extract from The Daily Telegraph Book of Obituaries by Martin Smith, published by Pan 2000; p154 Rough Guides Limited for an extract from The Rough Guide to Weather, published in 2002; pp155–156 The Met Office for 'The Great Smog of 1952', found on the Meteorological website.

Photographs: p11 Jess Coppell; p12 Corbis, Corbis, Getty; p15 Corbis; p24 Getty; p26 Hulton Getty, Alamy; p37 John Walmsley; p47 Corbis/Royalty free; p50 Catharine Hartley/ News International; pp57–58 Daily Mail Ski & Snowboard Magazine; pp78–79, 84, 104 Getty; p109 Allsport; p118 Hulton Getty; pp122–123 Lorne Campbell/Guzelian; p137 Alamy; p144, 146 Empics; p153 Hulton Getty; p154 Corbis; p155 Hulton Getty.

Tel: 01865 888058 www.heinemann.co.uk

Introduction

Developing Skills in Reading for KS3 Tests has been designed to help you develop your reading skills for the test at the end of Year 9. It will build on your strengths and help you identify areas that you need to improve.

This book contains stimulating texts for you to read and challenging activities to help you understand more about how texts work, with plenty of help and support to guide you. It also shows you how to write answers that will help you to get maximum marks in the test.

The book is divided into four sections:

Section A revises your understanding of different kinds of texts and how to respond to them effectively.

Section B equips you with all the reading skills you will need for the test.

Section C gives you practice in applying these skills to a wide range of text types. The 'Key Points' in each unit help you become familiar with the different techniques and effects that writers use and which you may be asked to explain in the test. Each unit can be used alone, or in groups of three texts which reflects the format of the actual tests. For each group of texts, there are also activities which allow you to practise comparing texts.

Section D contains information about the reading tests and guidance on how to give the best answers to the questions. There are also two practice tests which are just like the actual tests.

This book will help you to do well in your tests and will also provide a solid foundation for the future. More importantly, it will help you become a more skilful and perceptive reader – and that will enhance the rest of your life.

We hope you enjoy using this book and wish you every success in the tests, and beyond.

Andrew Bennett
Clare Constant

There are four types of boxes in this book to help make things clear.

 Help boxes contain information to help you with the questions on that page.

 Strategy boxes contain step-by-step instructions to help you do the activities.

 Remember boxes remind you of reading skills that will be useful in all your work.

 Key points boxes focus on techniques and effects that you may be asked to explain in the test.

Contents

A Revise

A1 Responding to texts — 8
- Reading an unfamiliar text
- Making sense of a difficult text

A2 Writing about texts — 16
- Summarising
- Using evidence from the text to prove your point
- Quoting from a text
- Referring to a text or a writer

B Skills

B1 Finding relevant information in a text — 22
Assessment Focus 1: Understand, describe, select, or retrieve information
- Understanding the question
- Skimming a text to gain an overview
- Scanning a text to find the key words

B2 Reading between the lines — 27
Assessment Focus 2: Deduce, infer or interpret information
- Drawing inferences
- Distinguishing between fact and opinion
- Recognising bias and objectivity
- Drawing conclusions

B3 Investigating how texts are put together — 34
Assessment Focus 3: Identity and comment on the structure and organisation of texts
- Appreciating the impact of how a text is presented
- Examining the way a text is organised

B4 Appreciating the writer's use of language — 40
Assessment Focus 4: Explain and comment on writers' use of language
- Responding to different registers
- Understanding the impact of literary features
- Understanding how atmosphere and mood are created

B5 Explaining the overall impact of a text — 47
Assessment Focus 5: Identify and and comment on writers' purposes and viewpoints and the overall effect of the text on the reader

C Practice

SNOW

C1   Snowball — 51
Poem: 'Snowball' by Carol Ann Duffy
Key points: Responding to a literary text

C2   Cliff jumping — 56
Instruction/explanation: 'Cliff jumping' by Martin Bell
Key points: Responding to a non-fiction text

C3   Snowboard — 61
Review: 'Amped: Freestyle snowboarding' by Lee Hall
Key points: Investigating how language is chosen for audience and purpose
Comparing texts: Commenting on structure, organisation and use of language

CHANGE THE WORLD

C4   Taken at face value — 66
Fiction: *Face* by Benjamin Zephaniah
Key points: Recognising how writers present themes

C5   Working angels — 71
Campaign letter: Ethiopiaid
Key points: Recognising how texts persuade

C6   Different worlds? — 77
Web page news report: 'Charity calls for "net-free" day'
Key points: Recognising the way web texts target their audience
Comparing texts: Understanding audience and purpose

NIGHT BEASTS

C7   Tiger! — 81
Fiction: *Secret Heart* by David Almond
Key points: Responding to a description

C8   Things that go scrunch in the night — 87
Literary non-fiction – autobiography: *Golden Bats and Pine Pigeons* by Gerald Durrell
Key points: Recognising how suspense is created

C9   Night flight — 92
Literary non-fiction – information/explanation text: *Life of Birds* by David Attenborough
Key points: Investigating how a text has been made entertaining
Comparing texts: Commenting on the way writers entertain their readers

BOXING CLEVER

C10 The present — 97
Fiction: *Sons of War* by Melvin Bragg
Key points: Investigating the techniques used to reveal a character

C11 Box below the line — 102
Media text – argument text: 'Boxing – blows below the collar only'
by John Worthington
Key points: Investigating how an argument is developed

C12 Spit or swallow? — 107
Persuasive/advice web text: 'The ultimate question: spit or swallow?'
by Flip Homansky
Key points: Investigating the way writers encourage readers to trust them
Comparing texts: Commenting on the writer's viewpoint

WHEN THE WAR IS OVER

C13 Home They Brought Her Warrior — 112
Pre-1914 poem: 'Home They Brought Her Warrior' by Alfred, Lord Tennyson
Key points: Investigating the theme in a pre-1914 text

C14 Defeat — 116
Reportage: *Tales by Japanese Soldiers* by Kazuo Tamayama and John Nunneley
Key points: Investigating a biased text

C15 Mum's Army — 121
Media text: 'How a Mum's army patrol …'
Key points: Investigating the way image is created in a media text
Comparing texts: Explaining bias in texts

WHO ARE YOU?

C16 Face to face — 126
Pre-1914 fiction: *Frankenstein* by Mary Shelley
Key points: Responding to the genre features of a text

C17 Sounds amazing — 130
Drama: *Pygmalion* by George Bernard Shaw
Key points: Investigating the culture revealed in a text

C18 Whose face is it, anyway? — 135
Scientific explanation: 'View from the lab' by Steve Jones
Key points: Appreciating the relationship a writer creates with the audience
Comparing texts: Explaining how writers entertain their readers

D Practice Tests

Preparing for the Key Stage 3 reading test — 140

Reading test 1 — 143
Literary non-fiction – autobiography: *On Trial* by Tony Adams
Fiction: *The Go-Between* by L. P. Hartley
Obituary: Lillian Board

Reading test 2 — 152
Fiction: *Bleak House* by Charles Dickens
Scientific explanation: *The Rough Guide to the Weather* by Robert Henson
Web page: 'The Great Smog of 1952'

REVISE
A1 Responding to texts

In this unit you will revise how to:
- read an unfamiliar text
- make sense of difficult words or parts of a text.

Reading an unfamiliar text

In the test you will be asked to read a text and answer questions about what it says and how it has been written. However, before you write anything, there are five key questions you should ask yourself to gain an overview.

1. **What is the text about?**
   Try to sum this up in a couple of sentences.

2. **What text type is it?**
   For example:

   fiction   *drama*   *poetry*   *argument*   *analysis*   *information*

    REMEMBER

   You may be told what text type you are reading on the test paper but if you are not, bear in mind that some texts are a mixture of text types, for example *explanation and analysis*.

3. **Who is the audience (the people who are going to read it)?**
   For example:

   teenagers   *small children*   *parents*   *the elderly*

4. **What is the purpose of the text (what is it trying to achieve)?**
   For example:

   to entertain   *to persuade*   *to inform*   *to explain*

5. **What are the features of the text? What do they suggest?**
   The text's features are the clues that will help you to understand more about the text and answer the test questions, for example:

   - presentational features – layout, pictures, use of fonts, colour and white space, etc.
   - organisational features – headings, paragraphs, conclusion, etc.
   - use of connectives, for example *but*, *and*, *because*, *so*
   - use of different sentence types – statements, questions, simple or complex sentences, etc.
   - range of vocabulary – formal, informal, technical, etc.

> Responding to texts

Activity 1

1. Work in pairs. Make a list of the different text types you have seen today and talk about how you recognised which text type each was. Use the five key questions on page 10 to help you.

   For example:
   An advertisement trying to persuade teenagers to buy a new mobile phone.
   It used a lot of different features, such as …

2. Now read the text on pages 10–11, and the annotations which show how you can apply the five key questions to an unfamiliar text you are reading for the first time.

3. What is the **a)** text type **b)** audience **c)** purpose **d)** features of the text below?

Shhh!

King Itztulowd had made a new law. Everyone had to be at home and asleep by 8.00 pm. As soon as it was 7.30 pm he snuggled into his royal
5 bed with a large mug of creamy hot chocolate and two munchy, crunchy chocolate biscuits. Then at 8.00 pm the Royal Flicker flicked the light switch and darkness fell. King
10 Itztulowd cuddled the royal teddy and that was it for the night. AND HE DIDN'T WANT TO HEAR ANOTHER SOUND TILL MORNING.

4. On pages 12–13 are some headings (A–C), photographs (D–F) and texts (G–I) that make up three different articles about teenagers.
   a Match the right heading, photograph and text to make three different articles.
   b Then decide who is the audience and what is the purpose of each article.

   Complete a chart like the one below with your answers. Then explain how you made your choices.

Article	Photograph	Text	Audience	Purpose
1				
2				
3				

9

A1: Revise

1 What is the text about?
This text is about the terrible conditions that battery hens live in. Free-range eggs cost only a little more than battery eggs. It wants the UK to ban battery cages.

2 What text type is it?
It's a persuasive text.

3 Who is the audience?
People who buy battery eggs.

4 What is the purpose of the text?
The purpose of the text is to persuade readers to stop buying battery eggs.

5 What are the features of the text? What do they suggest?

The heading tells readers the RSPCA's point of view.

'Intolerable' is a strong, emotive word that encourages readers to take the topic seriously.

The paragraphs are short and give facts and opinions.

'But hey …' Using informal English here means that this point arguing for battery hen farming doesn't carry as much weight as the points made in formal standard English.

This question challenges the reader to think about this issue.

Capital letters are used to make these words and numbers stand out.

The conclusion urges readers to act.

The layout is like a till receipt, which makes the reader think about shopping and buying eggs.

BATTERY CAGE CONDITIONS ARE APPALLING.

BUT, APPARENTLY, A FEW *PENCE EXTRA* FOR FREE-RANGE IS *INTOLERABLE*

OVER **20** MILLION HENS LIVE IN BATTERY CAGES IN THE UK. IF YOU CAN CALL IT LIVING. They're so crammed in that they can never open their wings.

And their bones can become brittle. But hey, their eggs can be a few pence cheaper than free-range.

SO DOES THAT MAKE IT JUSTIFIABLE?

Some people obviously think it does. Because, while **86%** of the British public say that battery cages are cruel, only **32%** of the eggs sold in Britain are barn or free-range.

AT THE RSPCA WE THINK THE UK SHOULD BAN ALL BATTERY CAGES AS SOON AS POSSIBLE. Margaret Beckett is considering it. So help her decide.

STOP BUYING BATTERY EGGS. FARM ANIMAL WELFARE. IT'S IN YOUR HANDS.

WWW.RSPCA.ORG.UK
Registered charity number 219099.

> Responding to texts

The picture of a boiled egg shows readers quickly what the text is about.

> A1: Revise

Heading A

Vote for Caxton's curfew

Heading B

Home time for teens

Heading C

Teen curfew could be on its way

Photograph D

Photograph E

Photograph F

> Responding to texts

Text G

Do you only dare venture out when it's broad daylight and the streets are crowded with families? Is it because you know mornings are the only time the town's yobbos are out of the way (sleeping off the late night they spent vandalising our town centre – again)?

Do you remember the good old days when you could leave your door unlocked and could walk home at midnight without a care in the world?

Do you want to reduce the amount of crime in our town?

If so, vote 'Yes' to a teenage curfew in Caxton town centre.

Text H

Teenagers want limits. Setting boundaries is one way of reassuring them that you care. Of course teenagers hate to admit this. So do not expect your teenager to shout 'hooray!' when you tell him or her what time to be home.

Times to be home by should be worked out bearing in mind these issues:

- How much sleep does your child need?
- What time are his or her friends expected to be home by? Do you think this is reasonable?
- Don't be sexist – treat girls the same as boys.

Text I

Mayor Megan East told B'Kool: 'In America over 200 cities have set curfews (times when teenagers have to be off the street). It is an idea that we are eager to try out here in Britain in an attempt to solve night-time youth crime, and to make our streets safer for older people to walk at night.'

In a recent survey of 13–17 year olds, 71% already had a set time when they had to be home. When asked, 75% of teenagers polled said it was unfair to have a curfew for all teenagers when only a very small minority caused problems.

What do you think? E-mail us here at B'Kool with your views.

 **Check!** Close your books and write down the strategy that will help you gain an overview of an unfamiliar text in the test.

> A1: Revise

Making sense of a difficult text

Activity 2

1   Work with a partner. What do you usually do when you don't understand a word in a text or a part of a text?

> **REMEMBER**
>
> → Try to pinpoint what is making the text difficult to understand. Is it a word? A sentence? Is the subject of the text difficult?
>
> → Use what you *do* understand to help you work out what you *don't* understand.
>
> → You do not need to understand every single word or detail in a text to answer the questions that you are asked in the test.

2   Read the strategies below. Then use them to help you work out the meaning of the underlined words, phrases and sentences on page 15.

Making sense of a difficult word

1   **Re-read the sentence and the paragraph that the word is in.**
    This will help you to understand roughly what the text around the word is about and will help you to guess what the word means.

2   **Look for parts of the word that you already know.**
    You may find that parts of the word are similar to words that you already know. This will help you to guess the meaning of a difficult word.

3   **Check the text for other uses of the same word.**
    Quickly read through the text to see if the word is used again elsewhere. Then use strategy 1 to give you more clues about the meaning of the word.

4   **Test your ideas.**
    Re-read the sentence and put in the meaning you think is correct. If it doesn't make sense, try again.

Making sense of a difficult part of a text

1   **Re-read the difficult part of the text.**
    Read each sentence slowly and carefully. After each sentence ask yourself: Who is doing what? What is happening here?

2   **Read the sentence or paragraph that comes *before* and *after* it.**
    Ask yourself: What did I find out? Then read the difficult part again.

3   **Look for clues and work out what they mean.**
    For example, you might find clues in the choice of vocabulary or connectives or punctuation.

4   **Rewrite longer sentences as shorter ones. Move clauses around.**
    This helps you to see the information in a new way, which might make it easier to understand.

> Responding to texts

3 Answer these questions, using the strategies if you need to.

    a Who is talked about in connection with a film called *Six Degrees of Separation*?
    b Explain the theory of 'Six Degrees of Separation'.
    c How was the experiment in the 1960s carried out?
    d What are researchers trying to test now?
    e Who is in charge of the research?
    f How is the new experiment going to be done today?

4 Which strategies helped you to answer questions 2 and 3?

Small world, isn't it?

Six Degrees of Separation: in the art world there is a film named after it and it's talked about in connection with Kevin Bacon, the actor. Now the science world is once again focusing on the phenomenon, and putting it to the test.

The theory is that everyone in the world knows everyone else via just half a dozen intermediaries. This claim was first referred to as 'Small World Phenomenon' and later led to the famous phrase 'Six Degrees of Separation', but after more than thirty years, nobody knows if it's true.

It all began with an experiment undertaken in the 1960s during which packages were sent to several hundred randomly selected people in Midwest America. Each recipient was asked to pass their parcel on to an individual in Boston, but only by the use of personal acquaintances likely to know the target person. On average the packages reached their destination after just six separate deliveries.

To investigate whether everyone in the world can be reached through a short chain of social acquaintances, a team at Columbia University is using e-mail to attempt a global version. Research leader Duncan Watts hopes to persuade at least 100,000 people to take part.

> From *Focus* magazine, June 2002

 Work in pairs. Close your books. Take it in turns to explain to your partner how to deal with a difficult word or difficult part of the text.

15

REVISE
A2 Writing about texts

When you answer questions about a text in the test, you may need to:
- summarise the main points or ideas in your own words
- use evidence from the text to prove the points you want to make
- quote parts of the text to support your points
- make it clear which text you are referring to, if you are writing about more than one text.

Summarising

Activity 1

1 Work with a partner.
   a Close your book and spend a few minutes discussing how you would sum up what a text is about.
   b Now compare your ideas with the three-step strategy below.

1 **Ask yourself: Why do I need to summarise this?**
   Once you have read the text and know the reason or purpose for your summary, you can decide what to put in and what to leave out.

2 **Scan the text and pick out only the key points you need.**
   When you scan a text, move your finger across the text as you search for key words. Only stop to read in detail what you need.

3 **Write the summary in your own words.**
   Don't copy out large chunks of the text: using your own words shows that you understand the text. It also allows you to make your point in fewer words, which saves you time.

2 Read the text on page 17. Following the steps above, write, in a couple of sentences, a summary that helps you answer this question:
   Why did William Spooner become famous?

   Remember to write the summary in your own words. You may like to start like this:
   William Spooner became famous for …

3 Work in groups and check each other's summaries. Make sure that:
   - all the information in the summary is needed
   - no important information is missing
   - the summary is in the writer's own words and has not been copied from the text
   - it is clear how William Spooner became famous.

   Give the best summary a grade A, the next best a grade B, and so on.
   Give reasons for your decisions.

Spoonerisms

The Reverend William Spooner was Warden of New College, at Oxford University from 1903 to 1924. He is not remembered as a great teacher (in fact, he was very boring), but he is remembered as an amazing word muddler. He used to mix sounds from different words as he was speaking
5 with hilarious results.

Once when Spooner was telling off a lazy student he said: 'You have hissed my mystery lectures. You have tasted a whole worm. You will leave Oxford by the next town drain.'

Another time Spooner visited an optician and had this baffling conversation:
10 SPOONER: Do you have a signifying glass?
OPTICIAN: No.
SPOONER: Well, it does not magnify.

One of Spooner's most famous muddlings happened when he was giving a talk and asked: 'Which of us has not felt in his heart a half-warmed fish?'
15 In the end, the way Spooner muddled his words became so famous it was given its own name: Spoonerism.

> A2: Revise

↘ Using evidence from the text to prove your point

When you are asked to explain something in a text you need to use details from the text to prove the points you want to make.

Activity 2

1. Brainstorm a list of words and phrases you can use when you want to explain what a small part of the text shows. For example:
   This quotation shows ...
   When the writer says ... it suggests ...

2. Read the example below. It shows you how to make good use of the text when you answer a question.
   Question: Would you like to have had William Spooner as a teacher?

1 Make a **point** that answers the question.

2 Give **evidence** from the text to prove your point. (This could be a quotation or a short summary.)

> I would not have liked William Spooner to be my teacher because the text says he was 'very boring', which suggests it would be hard to sit and listen to him.
> I prefer teachers who make lessons interesting.

3 Explain how the evidence you have given proves your point.

3. Now answer these questions about the text. Follow the steps:

   make a **point** → give **evidence** → **explain** the evidence

   a Why would Spooner's students have found him confusing?
   b Why didn't Spooner's conversation with the optician make sense?
   c Where does the term 'Spoonerism' come from?
   d Which Spoonerism did you find most entertaining?

 Work with a partner. Close your books. Take it in turns to tell each other how to use evidence from a text to prove your point.

> Writing about texts

↘ Quoting from a text

When you have made a point about a text, you can support your point by quoting from the text.

Activity 3

1. Work in pairs. Close your books for a few minutes and talk about how you would quote something from a text.

2. Quoting is quite simple if you remember the five rules explained in the example below.

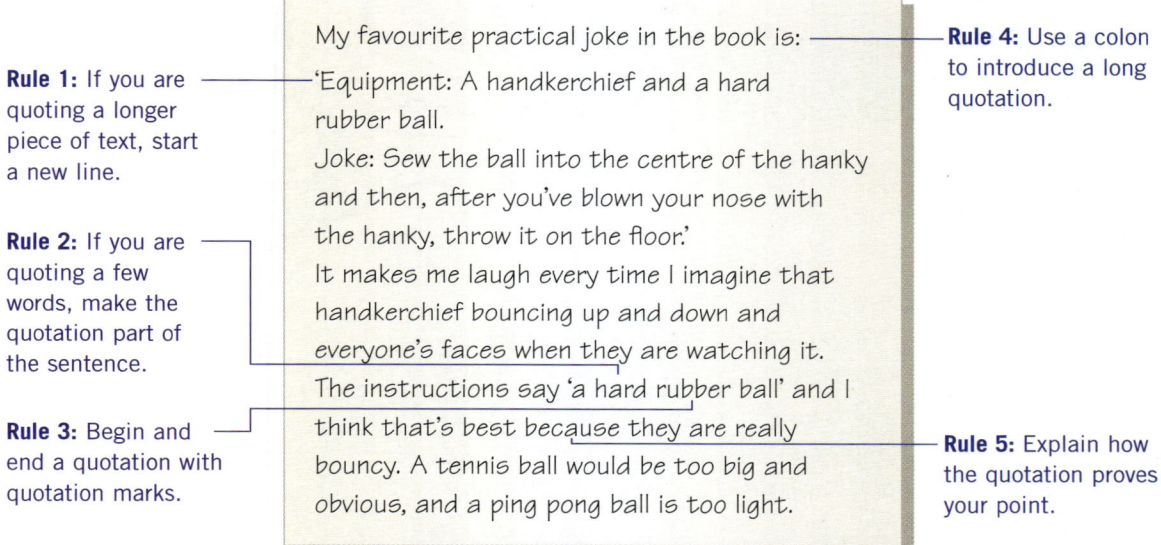

Rule 1: If you are quoting a longer piece of text, start a new line.

Rule 2: If you are quoting a few words, make the quotation part of the sentence.

Rule 3: Begin and end a quotation with quotation marks.

Rule 4: Use a colon to introduce a long quotation.

Rule 5: Explain how the quotation proves your point.

> ### REMEMBER
> Copy the text exactly. If you're copying part of a poem, begin a new line when the poet does.

3. Explain which of the practical jokes on page 20 you would like to play on someone and why. Write a short paragraph and use quotations in your answer. You could start like this: *The joke I'd like to play is …*

19

> A2: Revise

Joke 1

What you need: A tape recorder.
What you do: Record the theme tune of your friend's favourite TV programme. Then, wait till your friend is at your house watching TV. Every time they leave the room play the theme tune. Your friend will rush back in, thinking their favourite programme is about to start.

Joke 2

What you need: A raw, beaten egg and your friend's bottle of shampoo.
What you do: Pour the beaten egg into your friend's bottle of shampoo before they wash their hair. When they try to put hot water on their eggy head, the egg will scramble.

> From *The Silly Little Book of Practical Jokes*

4   Work in groups and check each other's writing. Tick their work as you make sure that:
- short quotations are part of the sentence
- long quotations start on a new line
- a colon has been used to introduce a long quotation
- the quotations have been copied correctly
- the quotation marks are in the right places.

5   There are four mistakes in the way the text has been quoted in the paragraph below. Can you find them?

My favourite practical joke in the book uses:
'yesterday and today's newspapers'. You have to 'swap the front pages of the two newspapers and keep the old newspaper with its new front page'.
My mum spent ages reading yesterday's newspaper before she said that they must be short of news because she remembered reading most of it yesterday. She couldn't work out why my sister and I were laughing so much.

> Writing about texts

Referring to a text or a writer

When you refer to a text or a writer, you should always make it clear to which text or writer you are referring. This is especially important when you discuss two texts.

Activity 4

1   Work in pairs.
    a   Close the book for a minute and discuss how you would write the title of a text and name of an author in a sentence.
    b   Now study the example below and see if you were right.

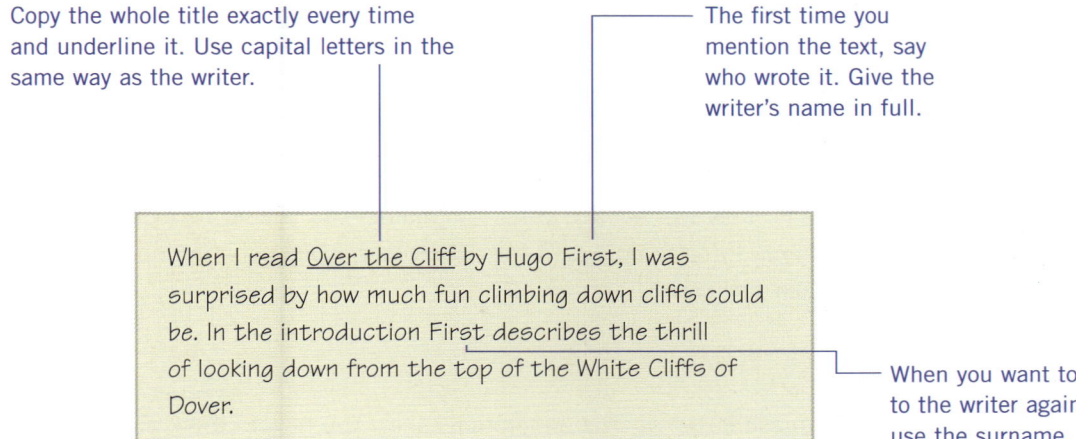

Copy the whole title exactly every time and underline it. Use capital letters in the same way as the writer.

The first time you mention the text, say who wrote it. Give the writer's name in full.

When I read Over the Cliff by Hugo First, I was surprised by how much fun climbing down cliffs could be. In the introduction First describes the thrill of looking down from the top of the White Cliffs of Dover.

When you want to refer to the writer again, just use the surname.

2   Write six sentences explaining which of these books you would give to your:
    a History teacher   c Head teacher   e school caretaker
    b R.E. teacher   d careers officer   f school cook

How Is Your School Doing?   A. Paul Ling
Mending Broken Chairs   Alan Dedonit
100 Best School Lunches   Arty Chokes
Know What You Want To Be   Toby Ornotobi
Robin Hood's World   Rob D. Rich
Suffering Saints   Helen Earth

 Work with a partner. Close your books and tell each other the three things to remember when you want to refer to a text or a writer.

21

SKILLS
B1 Finding relevant information in a text

In the test you will be assessed on your ability to find relevant information in a text so that you can answer questions about it. To do well at this sort of question you need to:
- understand what the question is asking you to do in order to score full marks
- skim the text: read it quickly to get an overview of the main ideas
- scan the text: search it quickly to find key words.

↘ Understanding the question

To get full marks on a question you need to answer it correctly. You need to look for the key words in the question – they will tell you what information you should be looking for. This may seem like a simple thing to do but in the actual test, when you are under pressure, it's easy to make a mistake.

Activity 1

1   Read the example question below. The annotations show you how to think about every part of the question before you answer it.

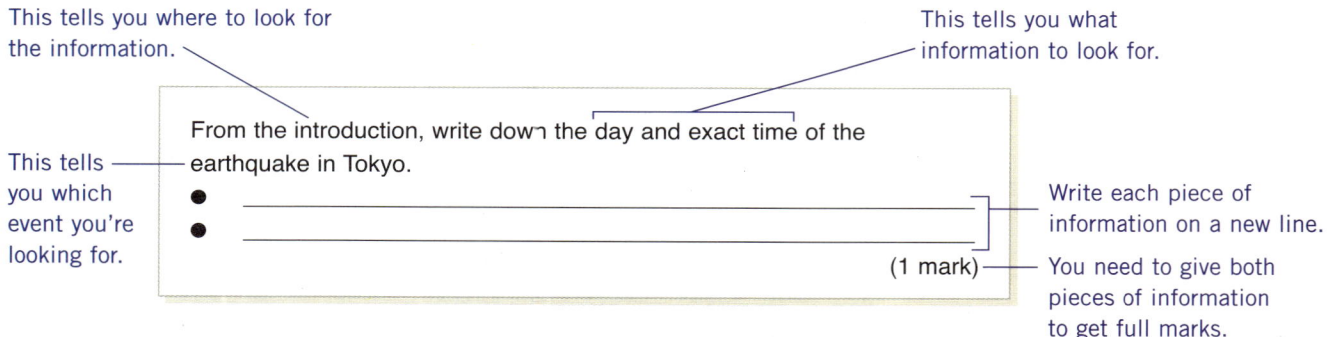

2   Read the questions below carefully. Decide:
- what sort of information you need to give to get full marks
- how you should write the answers.

Complete the chart below, giving one advantage and one disadvantage of having mobile phones in school.

Advantage	Disadvantage

(2 marks)

> Finding relevant information in a text

Explain one way in which paragraph 1 is an effective introduction to this article. Support your answer with a quotation.
___
___

(2 marks)

From paragraphs 3 and 4, identify three benefits of taking exercise three times a week.
- ___
- ___
- ___

(3 marks)

↘ Skimming a text to gain an overview

When you skim a text you read the whole text quickly to get an overview of the main ideas.

Activity 2

1 Work with a partner.
   a Close your books and share what you already know about how to skim a text.
   b Brainstorm a list of layout features that you might see in a text.

2 Now compare your ideas with this simple two-step strategy.

1 **Search the text for layout features.**
   The layout features (such as headings, pictures and italics) will give you clues to help you to work out what the text is about.

2 **Find the main points in the text.**
   Read:
   - the introduction (the first paragraph)
   - the first and last sentences of each paragraph
   - the conclusion (the last paragraph).
   Then sum up in your own mind what the main points are.

3 Look at the newspaper article on page 24 and the annotations showing how to search for clues in the layout features. Then quickly skim the first paragraph and answer this question:
   What did Walter Diemer invent?

4 Now skim the rest of the article and note down the main points made in each paragraph.
   Paragraph 2   *Walter Diemer invented bubble gum 70 years ago.*

5 In which paragraphs can you find the answers to these questions?
   a Why was the first bubble gum pink?
   b How did Diemer feel about his invention?
   c What is the name of the company that first made bubble gum?
   d How popular was Diemer's invention?

23

> B1: Skills

What clue does the heading give me as to what the article is going to be about?
It's about a famous man who has done something that has changed our streets.

The man who left his mark on history – and the world's streets

By Jay Iliff

At one time or another, Walter Diemer's legacy has been on the soles of everybody's shoes. No, he did not breed dogs; he invented bubble gum, thus earning himself an indelible place in history.

Diemer, who has just died at the age of 93, made his discovery 70 years ago. At the time he was a trainee accountant with the Fleer Chewing Gum Company in Philadelphia. In his spare time he began testing chewing gum recipes and accidentally came up with the new formula.

The fact that it was pink was also purely accidental – that was the only shade of colouring available to him.

Diemer's new product was an immediate hit. It was stretchier but less sticky than other formulas, and when he took a 5lb consignment to a local grocery shop it sold out the same afternoon.

The Fleer Company took over Diemer's recipe, called it Dubble Bubble and sold it in yellow wrappers at one penny a piece. Diemer was drafted in to help the sales drive, teaching the firm's salesmen how to blow bubbles for their demonstrations.

His wife Florence says: 'He was terrifically proud of it. He would say to me: "I've done something with my life. I've made kids happy around the world."'

And that was true: Diemer received hundreds of letters from children who loved bubble gum and – although he rarely chewed it himself – he would sometimes invite youngsters to his home where he would explain how he invented the gum and preside over bubble-blowing competitions.

He remained with Fleer until his retirement as senior vice-president in 1970 and also retained something of an eccentric quality. In his old age, he would ride through the streets around his home on a tricycle.

Diemer's invention never made him rich, as he received no royalties, but he bore no grudges. 'My gum was an accident,' he recently told an interviewer. 'I was doing something else, and ended up with something with bubbles.'

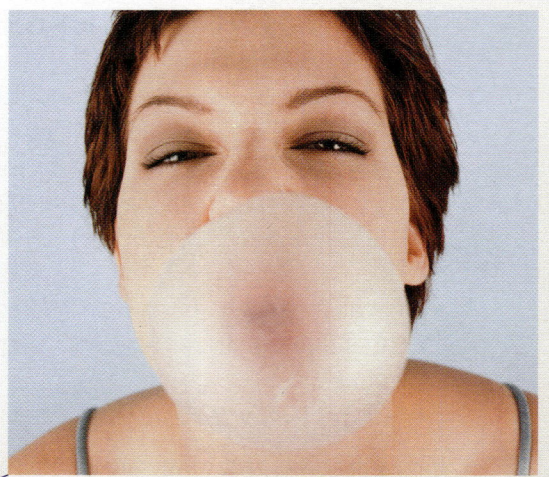

Burst of enthusiasm: children have ensured Diemer's invention remains popular

> From the *Express*, 14 January 1998

What do the caption and photo tell me about the topic of the article?
The article is going to be about the invention of bubble gum and how children enjoy it – perhaps competing to see who can blow the biggest bubble.

> Finding relevant information in a text

 ## Scanning a text to find the key words

Once you have read the question carefully and skimmed the text quickly to get an overview of the main ideas, you need to scan the text to find key words that will help you to find the details needed to answer the question.

Activity 3

1 Work with a partner. How do you usually go about scanning a text?

2 Of course, you can always find the information you want by reading the whole text line by line, but the following three-step strategy shows a quicker way, which is useful in the test.

1 Read the question carefully and work out exactly what you are looking for.

2 Skim the text to find out where the information is likely to be.

3 Scan those parts of the text like this student (on the test paper you can underline or highlight the key words).

I sweep my finger across line by line as I search for key words. I only stop when I see what I need. Then I make a note of it.

3 Work in groups. Scan the text on page 26 and write down what is on the menu for these meals.
    a 1952 Wednesday lunch   d 1952 Thursday lunch
    b 2002 Sunday tea   e 2002 Friday breakfast
    c 1952 Monday breakfast   f 1952 Snacks on Tuesday

4 Work on your own. Scan the text again and find out how often children ate vegetables in a) 1952 b) 2002.

 How can scanning help you in the test?

25

> B1: Skills

THE WEEKLY MENU

1952   2002

SUNDAY (1952)
- **Breakfast:** Boiled egg, two slices of toast, scraping of butter, tea with milk
- **Lunch:** Roast beef, Yorkshire pudding, roast potatoes, carrots, cabbage, apple pie, custard
- **Tea:** Bread and dripping
- **Snacks:** Ovaltine
- **DAILY TOTAL: 1,923 cal**

SUNDAY (2002)
- **Breakfast:** Sugared cereal, milk, orange juice
- **Lunch:** Steak, chips, baked beans, cola
- **Tea:** Spaghetti hoops on toast, chocolate bar
- **Snacks:** Nachos, salsa dip
- **DAILY TOTAL: 1,958 cal**

MONDAY (1952)
- **Breakfast:** Two slices of toast, scrape of butter
- **Lunch:** Beef stew, mashed potato, carrots, peas, spotted dick pudding, custard
- **Tea:** Bubble and squeak, tapioca
- **Snacks:** Apple, pear, Ovaltine
- **DAILY TOTAL: 1,943.5 cal**

MONDAY (2002)
- **Breakfast:** None
- **Lunch:** Tagliatelle, tomato and basil sauce, iced carrot cake, cola
- **Tea:** Pizza and oven chips, ice-cream, grapefruit squash
- **Snacks:** Two bags of crisps, sweets
- **DAILY TOTAL: 2,309 cal**

TUESDAY (1952)
- **Breakfast:** Cereal with milk, tea
- **Lunch:** Lamb hotpot, potatoes, peas, semolina
- **Tea:** Pork pie and salad
- **Snacks:** Teacake and butter
- **DAILY TOTAL: 2,080 cal**

TUESDAY (2002)
- **Breakfast:** Bag of crisps
- **Lunch:** Sausage, chips, tinned spaghetti, jelly, ice-cream, cola
- **Tea:** Sweet and sour chicken Chinese takeaway, fried rice, chocolate milk
- **Snacks:** Two chocolate snack bars
- **DAILY TOTAL: 2,434 cal**

WEDNESDAY (1952)
- **Breakfast:** Two slices of toast, scraping of butter, jam, tea with milk
- **Lunch:** Mutton stew, mashed potatoes, cabbage, carrots, rice pudding
- **Tea:** Offal, boiled potatoes, peas, green beans
- **Snacks:** Sweet biscuits
- **DAILY TOTAL: 1,966 cal**

WEDNESDAY (2002)
- **Breakfast:** Two slices of toast with margarine and chocolate spread
- **Lunch:** Fish fingers, chips, peas, summer fruit tart and custard, chocolate milk
- **Tea:** Spaghetti bolognese ready meal, slice of chocolate cake, orange squash
- **Snacks:** Bag of crisps
- **DAILY TOTAL: 2,186 cal**

THURSDAY (1952)
- **Breakfast:** Cereal with milk, tea with milk
- **Lunch:** Boiled beef, boiled potato, peas, green beans, stewed apple, custard
- **Tea:** Powdered egg omelette, fruitcake
- **Snacks:** Milk drink
- **DAILY TOTAL: 1,897 cal**

THURSDAY (2002)
- **Breakfast:** Cereal bar
- **Lunch:** Chicken nuggets, chips, fruit yoghurt
- **Tea:** Quiche, baked potato, butter, salad, cola
- **Snacks:** Two chocolate snack bars
- **DAILY TOTAL: 1,974 cal**

FRIDAY (1952)
- **Breakfast:** Boiled egg, two slices of toast, scraping of butter, tea with milk
- **Lunch:** Baked cod, chips cooked in lard, rice pudding
- **Tea:** Ham, cheese salad sandwich, jam sponge
- **Snacks:** Ovaltine
- **DAILY TOTAL: 1,930 cal**

FRIDAY (2002)
- **Breakfast:** None
- **Lunch:** Macaroni cheese, salad, ice-cream
- **Tea:** Chicken tikka masala ready meal, trifle, orange squash
- **Snacks:** Two bags of crisps, chocolate bar
- **DAILY TOTAL: 1,932 cal**

SATURDAY (1952)
- **Breakfast:** Two slices of toast, scrape of butter
- **Lunch:** Bacon sandwich, teacake with butter
- **Tea:** Corned beef, salad, bread and dripping
- **Snacks:** Liquorice sweets and pear
- **DAILY TOTAL: 1,864 cal**

SATURDAY (2002)
- **Breakfast:** Cereal bar
- **Lunch:** Cheese burger, chips, cola
- **Tea:** Instant noodles, jam tart, chocolate milk
- **Snacks:** Biscuits
- **DAILY TOTAL: 1,766 cal**

> From the *Daily Mail*, 31 May 2002

Word bank **offal** – the intestines, heart, kidneys, liver, etc. of an animal

SKILLS
B2 Reading between the lines

In the test you will be assessed on your ability to 'read between the lines'. As you know, this means that you need to look for clues in the text, work out what they mean, and then put all your ideas together to get at the true meaning of the text. To develop these skills you need to be able to:

- draw inferences from what you read
- distinguish between fact and opinion
- recognise bias and objectivity
- draw conclusions from what you have worked out.

Drawing inferences

Drawing inferences means working out what the details in a text hint at or suggest.

Activity 1

1. Talk in pairs. How do you usually go about working out what a writer is hinting at?
2. Read the two-step strategy below and look at the annotations around the text on page 28 to check if you were right about how to draw inferences.

1. Read the whole text so that you know roughly what it is about.
2. Read each relevant part of the text carefully. (It could be a word, a phrase, a sentence or a paragraph.) Then ask yourself: What does this suggest?

3. Read the text on page 28 quickly. In your own words, say briefly what it is about.
4. Now read lines 7–10. Complete a chart like the one below, drawing inferences about the four programmes Ned flicks to.

Programme	Evidence in the text	Reasons for my answer

5. Work in a group. Read the rest of the text. Make two more charts like the one above showing what you can find out about:
   a why Ned is annoyed
   b the person who phones.
6. Work alone. Use evidence from the text. Write four sentences explaining what kind of person Ned is and how he feels.

 REMEMBER

When you are asked to write about a text, remember to:
→ make your **point**
→ give **evidence** from the text to prove your point
→ **explain** how the evidence proves your point.

 Make a poster showing how to draw inferences.

27

> B2: Skills

Ned would like a sports car. The way he says this shows that he has a sense of humour because it's unlikely that a schoolboy would ever have such a car.

Has my McLaren F1 been delivered? Nope. Didn't think so.

Ned dumped his schoolbag by the door and stubbed off his old Nikes. Then he grabbed the remote, took a short run, and in one fluid movement crashed back onto the couch as he flicked on the TV.

'… get outta here. It's headed straight for us. We …'

'The bat in Patagonia …'

'Feeling hungry?'

'… you don't understand. He killed my brother. I've …'

An hour later, Ned was still watching aimlessly, prowling the channels. He watched a car chase to the ads, flicked to an air show, a jealous feud and back to the drama in the stolen car. He looked at the kitchen clock. Half past six.

Any minute now, he thought.

The phone rang.

Yep, she's been kidnapped again!

'Janet and Ned aren't home right now. Please leave a message.' Beep.

'Hello, Ned.' She knew he was there. Her voice was flat. 'Take the pie out of the freezer and put it in the oven, please. I'll be home around eight.' *Click.*

They force her to talk to prove she's alive.

Ten minutes passed. Then he heard the steady growl of the fax. He stood up and stretched. He was a lanky kid, not tall yet, but his loose limbs and big feet made you think of a puppy with large paws. He walked into his mother's study and ripped off the fax.

Could have guessed. Bet it's on email too. 'Take the pie out of the freezer and put it in the oven.' She bought ten, on special. Pie three nights in a row. That's seven pies to go. No vegetables. I wouldn't eat them, but they should be there.

The way Ned moves suggests that he is in a bad mood.

> From *Remote Man* by Elizabeth Honey

> Reading between the lines

Distinguishing between fact and opinion

Activity 2

1. Work in pairs. Close your books and answer this question: What is the difference between a fact and an opinion?

2. Now check your ideas against the information below.

A simple way to remember the difference between fact and opinion is:

1. **Facts** can be checked and proved.
   - *McLaren make racing cars.*
   - *Ned has a television at home.*
   - *Ned's mother works long hours.*

2. **Opinions** are someone's point of view.
   - *Ned shouldn't come home to an empty house every day.*
   - *Ned's diet is not varied enough.*

3. You can decide whether an opinion is **valid** or not by looking at whether it is backed up by evidence or reasons. A valid opinion might look like this:
   - *Ned's diet is not varied enough because he has had pie for three days running and hasn't had any vegetables with it.*

---

3. Work as a class. Read lines 1–9 of the playscript on page 30 and the annotations that show you how to decide what is fact and what is opinion. Why are the opinions valid?

4. Work as a group. Read lines 10–14. Make a note of two opinions and two facts. Tick any opinions that you think are valid.

5. Work on your own. Read the whole text and answer the following questions.
   a. What facts are you given about diet during the Second World War?
   b. Which opinions show that Julie and her Mum tease each other?
   c. Is Mum's opinion about tonight's dinner being 'real food' valid?

6. Work as a class.
   a. Everyone should write down one fact and one opinion on separate slips of paper and hand them to the teacher.
   b. Then the class should split into teams. The teacher reads out one of the facts or opinions, and each team has to guess whether it's a fact or an opinion.
   c. The team with the most correct answers wins.

> B2: Skills

Is this a fact or an opinion?
Is it possible to find out if this is true?
Yes, so this is a fact.

Is this a fact or an opinion?
The words 'far too much' show it's an opinion.

Six o'clock in the evening. Mum has just arrived home from work. Julie is sitting in front of the computer.

Mum Hello, I'm back ... Julie? Julie, at least say 'hello' when I walk through the door. What are you up to?

5 **Julie** Oh, hello. Mum, I'm doing my History project.

Mum That school gives you far too much homework. When I was at school we only had an hour a night. Then we had time to help our mothers get the dinner.

10 **Julie** Very funny. This is really interesting. It's all about rationing during the Second World War, when it was difficult to get food. The food then was disgusting. It makes your cooking look fantastic.

Mum People had a very healthy diet during the war – the
15 best diet this country has ever had. People ate loads of vegetables and very few sweets.

(*Looking over Julie's shoulder at the screen*)

Liver and onions followed by carrot custard sounds delicious. Perhaps I should go out and get some –
20 just to help you with your homework.

Julie Thanks, but I'd rather have a microwaved lasagne – again.

Mum No, no it's real food tonight.

Julie Oh, what is it?

25 **Mum** (*peering in carrier bag*) Reconstituted vegetables, hydrolysed protein and additives ... or we could have roast chicken with all the trimmings. Your dad has just put it in the oven.

Is this a valid opinion?
Yes, because Mum offers evidence to back up her opinion – Julie has more than an hour's homework to do every night compared with her Mum, who had only one hour when she was at school.

> Reading between the lines

Recognising bias and objectivity

Activity 3

1 Work as a class.
   a Discuss the two points of view in these speech bubbles and decide which is balanced and which is one-sided.
   b Talk about what makes someone's opinion fair or unfair.

Students could be paid to do homework. That might help some of them to make more effort. However, it would be expensive for schools and it might lead to copying and cheating.

Students should be paid to do homework. It's not fair that they have to work for free.

---

1 A **biased** view is one-sided. Biased texts are not trying to be fair. They look at a situation from one point of view and do not give the full picture.

2 An **objective** view is fair and balanced. Objective texts consider all points of view and try to give a full picture.

---

2 Now read the three letters to a newspaper below. Decide whether each one is biased or objective. How do you know?

3 How could you change the objective letter to make it biased?

4 Choose one of the biased letters. How could you change it to make it more objective?

Teenagers home alone

Dear Editor

There is increasing concern over the number of teenagers who come home from school to an empty house. Parents are working long hours and may not arrive home until seven or eight o'clock in the evening. But does this do any real harm?

Once teenagers reach 14 it is perfectly legal for them to be at home on their own. I believe having to take responsibility for doing their homework, preparing a meal, etc. can encourage greater maturity, independence and a sense of responsibility. We mollycoddle and protect our children too much. We are in danger of producing weak adults.

Yours sincerely
Professor A. Hardrow

Dear Editor

It is true that it is legal for teenagers to be home alone at 14 and that taking responsibility for doing their homework and preparing their own food encourages maturity and independence. However, teenagers can still do these things if there is an adult carer at home. Of course, many parents have to work long hours and it can be difficult for them to get home early but I think it is important that an adult carer is there to listen to teenagers and encourage them to get on with their homework.

Yours sincerely
Denzel Settle

Dear Editor

What about the evidence that teenagers who come home to an adult carer get better exam results? Most teenagers arriving home to an empty house are tempted to watch TV or ring their mates or go on the internet rather than do their homework.

Fourteen-year-olds are not adults yet, and even adults benefit from having someone around when they get in – to talk through their day and share their problems with. Having that kind of support will help teenagers become confident mature adults – not leaving them to sort everything out by themselves. If they have to wait till Mum gets in at eight o'clock, everyone is tired and the chance to really talk has been lost.

Yours sincerely
Comfort Lovekyn

31

> B2: Skills

↘ Drawing conclusions

In the test you may be asked to find several pieces of information in a text and work out how they link together so that you can draw conclusions from them.

Activity 4

1. You are going to answer this question using information from the extract on page 28, the playscript on page 30 and the letters on page 31:

   Use the three texts to show whether it is a good idea for teenagers to come home to an empty house.

   You will learn how to use the five-step strategy on the opposite page as you do the activities below.

2. Work as a class as you do steps 1–3 of the strategy.

3. Work in pairs as you do step 4 of the strategy. (Each of you should make your own chart.)

4. Work in a different pair. Check each other's charts by:
   - ticking each clue that seems sensible to you
   - putting a star by each conclusion that seems reasonable.

5. Work as a class. Use your charts to help you write a series of sentences using evidence from the text to prove your conclusions are reasonable. Use the example in step 5 to help you.

Check! Close your books and make a poster showing the strategy you would use to draw conclusions about a text.

> Reading between the lines

1. **Read the question carefully and work out:**
   - what you need to find out
   - where you need to look for the information.

2. **Scan the texts for *all* the information that is relevant to the question. Make notes in a chart like the one below.**

Story about Ned	Playscript about Julie	Letters about teenagers home alone
He comes home and watches TV. He doesn't do his homework.	She gets on with her homework. Her Mum gets home at 6.00 pm.	The first letter argues that it is acceptable for teenagers to come home to an empty house. Teenagers will …

3. **Find details that link up.**
   Look at your notes and draw a line between pieces of information that are about the same topic, as has been done in the chart above.

4. **Draw conclusions using the linked information.**
   - Decide what is similar and what is different.
   - Look for more clues in the text to help you explain the points you want to make and then draw your own conclusions.
   - It is useful to record your ideas in a chart like the one below.

Linked information	Clues in the text that tell you why this might be	Conclusions
Ned doesn't get on with his homework but Julie does.	This could be because: • Julie's Mum is home by 6.00 pm but Ned's doesn't get home till 8.00 pm. • Julie gets on better with her Mum than Ned does with his Mum. • Julie is more mature than Ned.	Some teenagers who are home alone will get on with their homework. It may be all right to be home alone as long as it's not for too long and the teenager is mature enough to cope.

5. **Write your conclusions.**

Make your **point** – one of your conclusions.

Give **evidence** to support it.

Explain how the evidence supports your conclusion.

> Some teenagers who are home alone will get on with their homework like Julie. Others like Ned will not. Ned's mother does not get home till 8.00 pm, whereas Julie's mother is home by 6.00 pm. So whether the teenager gets on with homework may depend on how long he or she is left alone.

33

SKILLS
B3 Investigating how texts are put together

In the test you will be assessed on your ability to explain how the way a text is organised helps it to reach its audience and achieve its purpose. You may be asked questions such as:

- What effect does the way the text is presented have on readers?
- How does the way the text is organised suit its purpose?

When you answer questions like these, you need to refer to the text in detail to support and explain the points you want to make.

 ## Appreciating the impact of how a text is presented

Activity 1

1. Brainstorm a list of presentational features you find in texts. Here are some ideas to get you started:

    pictures   layout of the text   captions   colour

2. Now think of some examples of real texts and the different presentational features you find in them. For example:

    a magazine article – colour, captions, big and small pictures

3. The text opposite is an advertisement for the National Canine Defence League. The audience for the text is animal lovers, especially dog lovers, and the text's purpose is to persuade people to give money to the NCDL.

    Work as a class. As you read the text, study the annotations around the text, which explain how the presentational features help the writer to reach the audience and achieve the purpose. In this text the main presentational features are to do with:
    - pictures
    - use of colour
    - size
    - layout
    - print

4. Work in a group. Look at the text on the opposite page and the text on page 37. Discuss what impact each of the presentational features has on the reader.

5. Work in pairs. Compare the texts on the opposite page and on page 37 and decide which makes most effective use of these presentational features:
    a colour
    b pictures
    c types of print
    d headings.

 Make a poster showing all the presentational features you might find in a text and the questions you should ask yourself about the impact they have on the reader.

34

> Investigating how texts are put together

How does the layout of the text persuade readers?

The layout is in the shape of two hearts linked together, with text on the left and the photo on the right, so that the whole looks like an open locket. The heart symbol appeals to readers' emotions, because it represents love.

What types of print are used? How do they contribute to the effect?

The white stands out from the red and attracts readers' attention.

The question is in a handwriting font, which makes it seem more personal.

The simple clear logo is black on white, and stands out against the red.

The black writing is used to pick out the dog's name, suggesting that money given to the NCDL would go straight to him.

How does the size of the picture help to persuade readers to give money?

By making the picture of the dog so big, the writer appeals to readers' emotions and emphasises the real dog that needs help.

How does this picture affect readers?

It shows an old dog. Readers will feel sorry for the dog and will want to help him.

What impact does the use of colour have?

It's bright red, which makes you notice it. Because it's like a red heart, it builds on the idea of loving dogs.

▷ National Canine Defence League

35

> B3: Skills

Examining the way a text is organised

Activity 2

1. Close your books. What features do you look for when you are thinking about the way a text is organised? Compare your ideas with the list of questions below.

> **REMEMBER**
>
> When you read a text, always ask yourself: *What is its text type, audience and purpose?* because this will influence the choices the writer makes.

Looking at the whole text

There are six key questions you should ask yourself when you're thinking about the organisational features of a text.

1. How do the titles and headings grab the reader's attention?
2. What does the introduction lead readers to expect?
3. What does the conclusion do? For example, does it:
   - sum up the text?
   - reach a conclusion?
   - make a final statement?
   - link back to the beginning?
4. What effect do the topic sentences have?
5. What link words and phrases are used and how do they work?
6. What connectives are used and how do they work?

2. Work as a class and look at the newspaper article opposite.
   a. Read the text quickly. What is its text type, audience and purpose?
   b. Now read the text again. As you read, study the annotations, which show how the six key features are used to organise a text.

3. Work as a group. Explain the impact of the way the NCDL advertisement on page 35 is organised. Make a note of your ideas in a chart like the one below.

Organisational feature	Why it suits the audience	How it suits the purpose
Title		

4. Work on your own. Think carefully about the two texts you have read. Decide which writer made best use of each of the six features to organise their text.

Check! Close your books. What are the six features that writers often use to organise their texts? Use the mnemonic **T**igers **I**n **C**ages **T**ease **L**azy **C**ubs to help you remember them.

> Investigating how texts are put together

How does the heading grab the reader's attention?
The words 'late shift' are usually used in connection with work at a factory, not a school so the reader will think that something unusual is going on here and will want to read on to find out more.

Happy on the late shift

What does the introduction lead the reader to expect?
It explains that this school had a problem with staff shortages but it has found a solution. The reader hopes to find out about the benefits of this set-up.

What do these topic sentences do?
They introduce different groups of people who are affected by the new start times.

What job does the link phrase 'another benefit' do?
It links the points together, adding to the idea that this is a success.

What does the connective word 'so' do?
It makes the ending idea sound like a result of what's gone before.

Staff shortages have led one school to take a more flexible approach to the school day – with happy results!

At Middleton High lessons begin at 8.15 am for Years 7 and 8, but not till 10.00 am for the rest of the school. Head Teacher Gary Becks explained: 'We realised that offering part-time teachers a better deal meant we could solve our staffing shortage. By staggering the start of the school day we've filled all our vacancies and it's had a positive effect on students.'

Parents of Year 7 and 8 students are pleased with the new arrangements. 'It's easier to drop the kids off before I go on to work in winter, and my child can be home before it's dark,' one Year 7 mum said. Aware that some families do not want their child returning home to an empty house at 2.30 pm, Middleton High offers a variety of after school clubs. 'More students spend time after school in the library and staff are reporting a real improvement in the quality of homework being done,' Gary Becks said.

For Years 9, 10 and 11 there has been a surprising benefit. Recent research has shown that melatonin (which makes humans go to sleep) does not start to work in teenagers till ten o'clock at night but they still need ten hours' sleep. Teenagers who go to bed at eleven need to sleep till nine o'clock to get a full ten hours' sleep – but have to make do with only eight hours' sleep if they get up at seven o'clock to go to school. Year 9 student Ben Morris said: 'After only eight hours' sleep I often felt grumpy and found it hard to concentrate. Now I can start school at ten I feel a lot better.'

Another benefit has been a reduction in bullying. 'There just seems to be less aggression around and less opportunity for trouble,' Gary Becks said. 'Generally students are happier – and that's got to be better for everyone.'

So maybe for older students at Middleton High those flexible school days really will be the happiest days of their lives!

Year 10 students at Middleton High beginning their school day

What job do the photo and the caption do?
They show that the text is about a school.

What does the conclusion do?
It plays on the old saying that 'schooldays are the happiest time of your life'. This links back to the beginning because the article is all about time.

37

> B3: Skills

Making sense of the way paragraphs are organised
Activity 3

1. Share what you know about the way paragraphs are organised in non-fiction. You could use these sentence starters:

   They usually begin with …   Some sentences will …   The last sentence …

2. Below is a four-step strategy you can use when you need to consider how a paragraph is organised. As you read the steps, look at the paragraph below.
   It is taken from the article on page 37 and the annotations show how to work out how the paragraph has been organised.

   1. **Remind yourself of the text type, audience and purpose of the whole text.**
   2. **Find and read the topic sentence.**
      Ask yourself: What is the main point of this paragraph?
   3. **Read each sentence that follows the topic sentence.**
      For each sentence ask yourself:
      a. How does it fit in with the main point? Does it provide evidence, examples, an explanation?
      b. Does the sentence add to the last point or contrast with it?
         (Hint: look for link words or connectives.)
   4. **Read the concluding sentence.**
      Ask yourself: What does it do? Does it:
      a. sum up the rest of the paragraph?   c. repeat a key idea?
      b. prepare readers for the next paragraph?   d. reach a conclusion?

The **topic sentence** is about the benefits of the new timetable for older students. It helps readers see how the change affects a particular group of people.

This sentence describes some research about teenagers and sleep. It introduces the benefit mentioned in the topic sentence.

This sentence explains more about the findings of the research.

Purpose and audience: this paragraph is from an information text for readers interested in how schools are run.

For Years 9, 10 and 11 there has been a surprising benefit. Recent research has shown that melatonin (which makes humans go to sleep) does not start to work in teenagers till ten o'clock at night but they still need ten hours' sleep. Teenagers who go to bed at eleven need to sleep till nine o'clock to get a full ten hours' sleep – but have to make do with only eight hours' sleep if they get up at seven o'clock to go to school. Year 9 student Ben Morris said: 'After only eight hours' sleep I often felt grumpy and found it hard to concentrate. Now I can start school at ten I feel a lot better.'

In this sentence, Ben's comment provides an example from real life to support the point being made.

The **concluding sentence** repeats a key idea – Ben's comment proves that the topic sentence is true.

3. Work in groups. Comment on the way the other paragraphs in the text on page 37 are organised to suit the purpose and the audience.

Check! Work with a partner. Explain the four-step strategy you can use to work out how a paragraph is organised.

> Investigating how texts are put together

Recognising the impact of the way a sentence is organised

You have looked at how whole texts and paragraphs are organised so that you can explain how they work. Even at the level of the sentence, writers try to make every word count so that they will reach the intended audience and achieve their purpose.

Activity 4

1 Work in pairs. Make a list of the five different types of sentences and write an example of each sentence type. Complete a chart like the one below.

Type of sentence	Example
Statement	
Question	

2 Read the example below to find out how to explain the impact of the way a sentence is organised.

1 What is the text type, purpose and audience of the whole text?
This sentence is from an information text for readers interested in how schools are run.

2 What kind of sentence is it?
It is a statement and gives an opinion.

> On the one hand I like not having to get to school till ten – but on the other hand I don't finish school till 4.40 pm.

3 What effect does the sequence of clauses have?
Try moving clauses around to see why the writer chose to put them in this order. The link words at the beginning of the first clause warn the reader that there will be a second point that balances out the positive point.

4 What job is the punctuation doing?
The dash makes it sound less formal and helps to emphasise the problem caused by starting the school day later.

3 Discuss the effect of the way the following sentences are written.
   a Before the change to the timetable, Rosie in Year 10 used to truant, but now she's at school every day.
   b Would you like your school to be run like this?
   c However late we start the school day, some students will always be late.

Check! Close your books and list the four questions you should ask when you are thinking about the way a sentence is organised.

SKILLS
B4 Appreciating the writer's use of language

In the test you may be asked to respond to the writer's use of language.
You may be asked questions such as:
- What register is used and what effect does it have?
- What effects have been created by the use of literary features?
- How has a particular atmosphere or mood been created?

When you answer questions like these, you need to:
- read the text carefully, looking out for details that will support your answer
- use quotations from the text to help you to explain how the effect is created.

↘ Responding to different registers

As you know, people use different registers – formal or informal, standard or non-standard English – in different situations and for different reasons. Writers may choose a certain register to create an effect, for example to be humorous or to show whether a person is friendly or pompous.

Activity 1

1. Brainstorm a list of situations where you would expect to hear different registers of English, for example:
   - people chatting at a party using informal English
   - lawyers in a court using formal, standard English.

2. Study the cartoon and strategy opposite to find out how to explain the impact of the different types of English used.

3. Work in a group. Study the zookeeper's second and third thought bubbles and for each one, decide:
   a. What sort of English is he using?
   b. How does that sort of English make him sound to readers?

4. Work on your own. Which of these three speeches do you think the zookeeper should make to his boss? Why?

5. Work as a class.
   a. How can you work out whether a text is formal or informal, standard or non-standard English?
   b. Brainstorm a list of impressions that the different sorts of English can be used to create, for example:

   Informal, non-standard English can make someone seem ...

> Appreciating the writer's use of language

1 It ain't my fault if he's took poorly bad. He done it to himself. I didn't ask him to eat them bars of soap. He must've thought they was chocolate 'cos of the smell. Get the vet to him quick!

2 In my estimation the elephant has suffered no significant ill-effects from having consumed three bars of soap. However, this is sufficient quantity to make observation by the vet advisable.

3 Max looks healthy enough but he has just eaten three bars of soap so I'd like the vet to check him over, just to make sure that he's all right.

Investigating different registers

1. **Work out what the situation is.**
   The zookeeper is talking to his boss.

2. **Find words that show whether the zookeeper uses formal or informal English and standard or non-standard English.**
   Abbreviated words like 'didn't' and non-standard words like 'ain't' and 'poorly bad'. The speaker uses non-standard verb forms such as 'took' non-standard verb forms such as 'took' instead of 'taken', 'done' instead of 'did' and 'was' instead of 'were'.

3. **Is this how readers would expect someone to speak in this situation?**
   No, the zookeeper should be trying to sound more formal.

4. **How does the writer's choice of language make the speaker sound?**
   Having the zookeeper speak in informal and non-standard English in this situation makes readers think he is not trustworthy or clever enough to be doing his job.

> B4: Skills

⤵ Understanding the impact of literary features

In the test you may be asked about the writer's use of literary features and their effect on the reader, especially in fiction or poetry. Using the correct terms to describe the literary features will help you to write a better answer to these questions.

Activity 2

1 Look at the chart below.
   a Match the literary features listed 1–8 with the correct definitions listed A–H.
   b Then think of your own example for each one.

Literary feature	Definition
1 Alliteration	A An object is described in language that relates to humans, e.g. *The wind whistled through the hole in the door.*
2 Metaphor	B Words, phrases or sentences are repeated, e.g. *It was a dark, dark forest.*
3 Simile	C One thing is compared with another, often using the words 'like' or 'as', e.g. *The building fell like a pack of cards.*
4 Personification	D Words whose endings sound the same, e.g. *driven* and *forgiven*.
5 Onomatopoeia	E A regular beat or a pattern of sounds, which can be achieved in different ways, e.g. through repetition or the sounds of words, e.g. *tick, tock, tick, tock.*
6 Repetition	F The sound of a word is associated with its meaning e.g. *buzz, hiss, rustle.*
7 Rhythm	G One thing is said to be another, e.g. *He was a giant on the football field.*
8 Rhyme	H Words whose beginnings sound the same, e.g. *Chancer's Chewy Toffee.*

2 Read the poem 'The Locust' opposite. Read the annotations, which point out two examples of literary features, and explain how they work in the text.

3 Now find other examples of literary features in the poem, and ask yourself these questions about each one:
   • Which literary feature is it?
   • What does it mean?
   • What effect does it create?

Check! Work in pairs. Close your books. Make a flow diagram showing how you can work out the impact of a literary feature.

| First ... | → | | → |

> Appreciating the writer's use of language

The Locust

1 **Which literary feature is it?**
This is a metaphor.

2 **What does it mean?**
It compares the locust's head with a grain of corn.
It suggests that they are both small, oval and a creamy colour.

3 **What effect does it create?**
It helps readers who may never have seen a locust to get an idea of what it looks like. It emphasises that although the locust is small, it can cause a lot of harm.

What is a locust?
Its head, a grain of corn; its neck, the hinge of a knife;
Its horns, a bit of thread; its chest is smooth and burnished;
Its body is like a knife-handle;
5 Its hock, a saw; its spittle, ink;
Its underwings, clothing for the dead.
On the ground – it is laying eggs;
In flight – it is like the clouds.
Approaching the ground, it is rain glittering in the sun;
10 Lighting on a plant, it becomes a pair of scissors;
Walking, it becomes a razor;
Desolation walks with it.

Anon

The repetition of this word seven times connects the short sentences that describe the locust. It creates a kind of rhythm or beat, which pulls the reader into the poem.

43

> B4: Skills

↘ Understanding how atmosphere and mood are created

If you are asked in the test to comment on how an atmosphere or a mood is created in a piece of fiction or a poem, look for details that will help you to work out the answer. For example, search the text for details about:

- sights
- sounds
- smells
- tastes
- the weather
- what people do
- what people say
- how people feel.

When you find a detail, look at the writer's choice of words and ask: What sort of feeling does this word suggest?

Activity 3

1 Work as a class.
   a Read text A and the annotations opposite, which show some of the ways in which the writer has created the atmosphere.
   b What other details can you identify that help to build up the atmosphere?

2 Work in a group. Read text B on page 46 and answer these questions:
   a What kind of atmosphere has the writer has created?
   b How has he achieved it?
   c How is the atmosphere different from that in text A?

3 Work in pairs. Choose one of the texts. How would you change it to create a completely different atmosphere? Use your ideas to rewrite the text.

Check! Work in pairs. Draw a mind map to help you remember what sort of details can be used to create atmosphere or mood.

44

> Appreciating the writer's use of language

1 **What does this opening sentence suggest?**

It introduces a positive atmosphere. When you read on, the details that follow add to this idea.

2 **What do these phrases suggest?**

They suggest that this street is a happy place.

In this extract from *Don't Open Your Eyes*, the writer describes the street where the character Diesel lives.

Text A

It was exactly the right kind of street. Nothing too posh or scary, but *nice*; a street where black and brown and white people lived together and nobody worried. Where people smiled as they walked by, where toddlers
5 sat on the kerb and played with their toys; and on Sundays everyone would come out with buckets and suds to clean their friendly, shabby cars. No one was cleaning a car this afternoon, but a young couple, man and a woman, were doing some work on theirs, with
10 tools laid out on the pavement. Diesel could hear them chatting to each other in happy, easy-going voices.

> From *Don't Open Your Eyes* by Ann Halam

3 **What does this detail suggest?**

Small children are playing on the street so it must be safe.

4 **Which other details create the same feeling?**

These words suggest happiness, too.

45

> B4: Skills

In this extract from the novel *Ghost behind the wall*, David has climbed into the ventilation system of his flat.

Text B

David wriggled on, another metre, then a bit more, then a bit more and the floor beneath him suddenly ended and he was staring down a pit, a terrifying pit that plunged down into an unearthly, bottomless darkness. He could so easily have fallen down! It was another pipe, a
5 downpipe, bigger than the pipe he was in. It tipped straight down further than his torch could reach. He gulped and tingled all over with fear. The drop made him sick but he couldn't help himself. He took the torch between his fingers and dangled it over the edge. He let his grip go loose. The torch swung in between his fingers. How horrible it
10 would be to have no light!

> From *Ghost behind the wall* by Melvin Burgess

SKILLS
B5 Explaining the overall impact of a text

In the test you will be assessed on your ability to explain the overall impact of a text. You may be asked to:
- identify and comment on the writer's purpose and viewpoint
- explain the writer's choice of language
- explain the effect of the text on its readers.

These questions carry most marks on the test paper.

Activity 1

1 Read the text below. What is its a) text type b) audience c) purpose?

One alarm clock it's very hard to ignore!

All these modern digital alarm clocks are all very well – but if you're one of these people who simply refuses to wake up to apologetic buzzers, polite bleepers or gentle music, you need something a bit more … well, robust. Let's face it, the only thing that will stir the dedicated lay in bed is an old-
5 fashioned ear-piercing bell-ringer. This great <u>little clock</u> gives you exactly that, with a <u>funky metallic blue case</u>, <u>big bold backlit luminous dial</u> and <u>luminous hands</u> into the bargain. But
10 the *pièce de résistance* is hidden inside – <u>two inset chromed bells</u> that <u>deliver a choice of 'loud' or 'extra loud' rings</u>. If anyone can
15 sleep through that, send the clock straight back and we'll refund your money without question (we will also be truly amazed).

20 *Uses 2 × C batteries (not supplied) 13 cm high.*
TWIN BELL ALARM CLOCK
£14.99 ML0097

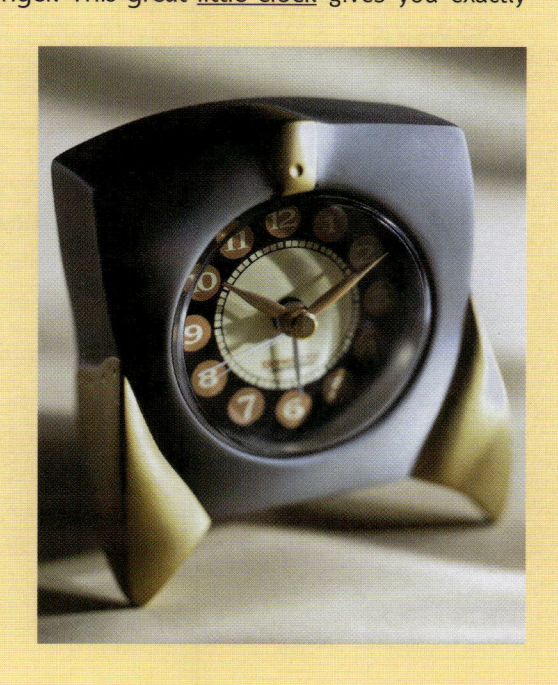

47

> B5: Skills

2 Below is an example of a question about the text on page 47, that you might find in the test. Read the following steps and find out how to plan your answer.

Preparing a detailed answer

Step 1 Read the question and decide which features of the text you need to look out for.

How effectively does the advertisement on page 47 persuade readers to buy the alarm clock? You should consider:
- the way the advertisement is presented
- what you are told about the alarm clock
- the variety of sentence structures used
- the writer's use of language.

- Look for presentation features such as headings, pictures, colour, print, etc.
- Look for facts, opinions, etc.
- Look for simple and complex sentences, questions, etc.
- Look for descriptions, literary features, formal/informal English, etc.

Step 2 Read the text and make notes as you read.
You may find it helpful to make notes in a chart like this:

In column 1 list each feature of the text that you are told to write about.

Make notes in column 2 on each feature, bearing in mind each point (underlined) of the main question.

Features of the text	How effectively does the text persuade readers to buy the alarm clock?
The way it is presented Headings, pictures, colour, print, etc.	The heading is effective because it boasts that this clock is different.
What you are told about alarm clock	
Variety of sentence structures used	
The writer's use of language	

Step 3 Use your notes and keep referring to the text as you write your answer.

For example:

- **the way the advertisement is presented**

The heading grabs readers' attention in two ways. First because it is in large black print and second because it suggests that the writer knows that the reader is able to ignore the alarm clock he or she has got at the moment. Readers who manage to ignore their alarm clocks are going to wonder what is different about this one – and if they read on and believe it can overcome that problem, then they are likely to buy it.

48

> Explaining the overall impact of a text

3 Now use the same strategy as you practise a similar type of question. Follow the instructions on page 48.

> **REMEMBER**
> → Make sure you answer each part of the question in the test.
> → Refer to the question in the answer.
> → Make sure you make a point, give evidence to prove it, and explain how the evidence proves your point.

a Work as a class. Use step 1 of the strategy to make a planning chart like the one on page 48 that will help you answer this question fully.

> How has the writer of the article on page 50 made sure that the opening to her account of her trip to the North Pole is entertaining while encouraging readers to read on?
> You should consider:
> - how she begins and ends this part of the text
> - the situations she describes
> - what kind of person she seems to be
> - her use of language.

b Work in groups using step 2 of the strategy. Spend 5–10 minutes planning an answer to the question.

c Work on your own and using step 3 of the strategy write your answer to the question. As you work:
- make sure that you keep answering the main question
- begin a new paragraph for each new point
- remember to support your points using quotations and details from the text, and to explain how the text proves your point.

You may find these sentence starters helpful:
The writer tells readers … This suggests … because …
Telling readers the fact that …. creates the impression that she is … because …

4 Work in a different group and mark each other's answers. Grade the best answer A, the next best B, and so on. As you consider each answer, look at whether:
- each part of the question is covered
- points are supported using quotations from the text
- the writer has shown how any quotations or details from the text prove the point being made
- the writer has answered the main question.

Check! Work in pairs. Close your books. Take it in turns to explain how to go about answering the longer question in the test.

Bridget Jones Goes to the Pole

by Catherine Hartley

My mother was driving me to Heathrow when I realised I hadn't any gloves for my trip. Normally this wouldn't have been a crisis, but this was different – very different.

I was on my way to walk to the South Pole, and even with my limited knowledge of Antarctica I knew that I had to keep my hands warm if I didn't want them to drop off with frostbite.

We were running late, crawling along Kensington High Street, but I spotted a sports shop and dashed in while Mum waited on a double yellow line.

In the calmest voice I could muster I explained to the salesman that I was on my way to join a polar expedition. It promised to be a very long, very cold journey and I needed the warmest and best gloves known to man.

Oh, and my plane was probably already on the tarmac with its engines revving.

If only there had been time, I could have added that I hated the cold, had terrible circulation and was one of those girls who hibernated under the duvet in winter.

But the assistant was already looking alarmed and when he mumbled something about the mountaineering section, I ran off to grab the most expensive gloves I could find, threw money at him and fled back to Mum's clapped out Mini Metro.

We set off again but the traffic got even heavier and the car began stalling at every junction. In a panic I jumped out at Hammersmith to take the Underground while Mum drove on with my luggage in the hope of meeting me at the check-in desk.

Somehow, we both managed it with minutes to spare, just in time for me to have to pay £150 in excess baggage. Then I ran to the departures gate and straight on to the plane for Punta Arenas, in southern Chile, for my last staging post before I set out across the ice.

I was off on the greatest adventure of my life. And frankly, I felt as petrified as a rabbit caught in headlights.

PRACTICE
C1 Snowball

In this unit you will practise responding to a poem you have not seen before. Read the poem on page 53 first, then find out how to use the four steps described opposite to help you make the most of the reading time in the test.

KEY POINTS

Responding to a literary text

When you are asked to respond to a literary text, it's not just what the writer says or even the special effects you notice that matters. You also need to be able to pinpoint the effect created by the writer's choices.

1   a   How do you go about reading a literary text for the first time?
    b   What do you look for when first reading a poem?

2   It helps when you are doing the test if you try to notice the sorts of things you are likely to be asked about as you read a literary text for the first time. Read the extract from the poem 'Snowball' and the four steps on page 52 to find out how to make sure you do this. Try out each step for yourself as you answer the questions.

3   a   Get into groups of four (this is your home group) and decide who will be A, B, C and D. Each of you should join your letter's expert group and study your part of the poem on page 53.
Expert group A studies lines 16–26.
Expert group B studies lines 27–33.
Expert group C studies lines 34–42.
Expert group D studies lines 43–55.

    b   Working in your expert group, each of you should copy and complete your own chart like the one below as you follow the four steps opposite and discuss your part of the poem.

Lines	What it's about	Poetic devices	Effect on reader

    c   Now return to your home group and take it in turns to read and explain your part of the poem to the rest of your group.

    When you listen, grade each speaker for how thoroughly they explain:
    - what the poem means
    - the effect on the reader of the poetic devices that the writer used.

Check! Work in pairs. Close your books and take it in turns to explain the four steps to each other.

> C1: Practice

Step 1 Keep pausing to sum up what is happening as you read.
In the test you will have to show that you have understood what the text is about, and that you can find pieces of information in it.

Question 1: What is happening in lines 5–8?

Step 2 Think about the details.
Ask yourself: What does this detail suggest or hint at?
In the test you will have to show that you can pick up on what the writer is hinting at by reading between the lines.

Question 2: What does the word 'sprats' in line 8 suggest?

> 5   Andrew Pond and Davy Rickers and me
>
>   went out,
>
>   three sprats, into the white bite of the world.
>
>   We shared my balaclava.
>
>
>   And for an hour we chucked snowballs
> 10 at the windows on our estate;
>
>   spattered the pristine panes of Nelson Way,
>
>   powdered the gleaming glass up Churchill Drive,
>
>   until we got bored
>
>   and Andrew Pond's mitts from his Granny
> 15 shrank.

Step 3 Look at the way the text is organised. Ask yourself: How does each feature add to what the text is about?
In the test you will be asked about the way the writer has organised the whole text and parts of the text such as paragraphs or sentences. When you are reading a poem this means noticing:
- any patterns that are used, e.g. regular rhyme schemes, rhythm, length of stanzas
- contrasts, such as dark and light, cold and hot, happy and sad
- the order in which information is given, e.g. in complex sentences.

Question 3: What is the contrast in mood shown in these lines from the poem?

Step 4 Search for special effects the writer has used. Pinpoint *how* they are created and *why* they are effective.
In a poem this means you must look for any images the writer uses. What is compared? Is it apt?

Question 4: Why are the images in line 8 effective?
You also need to listen to the sound of the lines in each stanza. Pinpoint what effect each sound has and why it is used.

Question 5: How do the sounds in lines 8 and 11–12 bring to life what is happening?

52

> Snowball

The poem 'Snowball' by Carol Ann Duffy describes what happened in her childhood when she and her friends made a huge snowball.

Snowball

More snow fell that week
than had fallen for thirty years.
The cold squeezed like a bully's hug
and made you grin at nothing.

5 Andrew Pond and Davy Rickers and me
went out,
three sprats, into the white bite of the world.
We shared my balaclava.

And for an hour we chucked snowballs
10 at the windows on our estate;
spattered the pristine panes of Nelson Way,
powdered the gleaming glass up Churchill Drive,
until we got bored
and Andrew Pond's mitts from his Granny
15 shrank.

It was me who started it off,
that last snowball,
rolling it from the size of a 50p scoop,
down Thatcher Hill,
20 to the size of a spacehopper.
It creaked under my gloves as I pushed.
Then Dave Rickers and Andrew Pond joined in,
and we shoved the thing
the length of Wellington Road.
25 It groaned as it grew
and grew.

The size of a sleeping polar bear.
The size of an igloo.
The size,
30 by the time we turned the corner
into the road where I lived,
of a full moon –
the three of us astronauts.

The worst of it was
35 that Andrew Pond and Davy Rickers ran off,
leaving me
dwarfed and alarmed
by a planet of snow
on our front lawn.
40 It went so dark in our living room,
I was later to hear,
that my mother thought there had been an eclipse.

And later that night –
after the terrible telling-off,
45 red-eyed,
supperless –
I stared from my bedroom window
at the enormity of my crime,
huge and luminous
50 under the ice-cold stars.
To tell the truth,
It was pride that I felt,
even though
I had to stop in for as long as it took
55 for the snowball to melt.

Carol Ann Duffy

Word bank
sprats – small fish

> C1: Practice

HELP | Types of questions

The questions you are asked below focus on different types of reading skills.
- Questions 1–2 require you to select information from the text.
- Question 3 requires you to 'read between the lines'.
- Question 4 requires you to look at why the writer has structured and organised the text in a particular way.
- Question 5 requires you to investigate the writer's language choices.
- Question 6 requires you to look at the overall effect – how the writer's choices affect a reader's response.

Questions

1 Name two pieces of clothing that the children have with them.   *(1 mark)*

REMEMBER

You must make enough points in your answer to earn each mark, for example, to earn 1 mark in question 1 you must name *both* the pieces of clothing. To earn 1 mark in question 2 you must find and copy out the names of *four* places.

2 Which four places do the children pass through?   *(1 mark)*

3 From lines 41–55, explain the difference between the way the poet and her mother feel about the snowball. How can you tell?   *(3 marks)*

HELP | Comparing characters

You can use the following strategy to help you to compare characters' feelings.

Step 1 Work out how each character feels.
- What do they say, think and do? How do they look (frowning, smiling, etc.)?
- What does this suggest about the way they feel?

Step 2 Compare the characters' behaviour and feelings.
- What is the same?
- What is different?

4 Re-read lines 29–33 below. How does the way the sentence is written add to the feeling of surprise at how the snowball grew?

> The size,
> by the time we turned the corner
> into the road where I lived,
> of a full moon –
> the three of us astronauts.

(2 marks)

54

> Snowball

? HELP | How a sentence is organised

When you are asked to look at how a sentence is written, notice the order in which information is given and ask yourself:
- What information is given first and what is held back until the end?
- What effect does holding back this information create? For example, does it build suspense, or create an element of surprise; does it act like the punchline of a joke?

5   Explain how each of the following images adds to the humour of the poem.

   a   three sprats, into the white bite of the world (line 7)   *(1 mark)*

   b   the size of a spacehopper (line 20)   *(1 mark)*

   c   the size of a sleeping polar bear (line 27)   *(1 mark)*

   d   the size of an igloo (line 28)   *(1 mark)*

6   How has the writer made the story of the snowball entertaining?
    You should write about:
    - what happens to the writer
    - the writer's choice of names and places
    - the way the snowball is described
    - the way the writer uses exaggeration.   *(5 marks)*

55

PRACTICE
C2 Cliff jumping

In this unit you will practise responding to a non-fiction text that you have not read before. Read the text on page 58 first, then find out below how having a checklist of the sort of things to look out for will help you to make the best use of the reading time in the test.

KEY POINTS

Responding to a non-fiction text

1. a Work in groups. Brainstorm a list of features to look out for when you are reading a non-fiction text.
   b Work as a class. Compare the lists from each group and put together a complete list of non-fiction features to try to spot.

In the test you will be asked to read non-fiction texts and write about the impact of the features the writer has used. This is why it makes sense to work out what text type you are reading, its purpose and its audience when you start reading. Then, as you examine the features the writer has used, you can decide how effective they are at reaching the chosen audience and helping the text achieve its purpose.

2. Read the example opposite, which is taken from an article about cliff jumping, and find out how to examine the features of a non-fiction text.

3. Work in groups. Read the article on page 58 again and talk about how the four features below help the text to:
   a appeal to less experienced skiers
   b encourage readers to try cliff jumping.

   Features
   - The type of print and font used for headings.
   - The choice of describing words in the headings.
   - Starting each of steps 1–5 with an adverbial phrase ('Skiing towards the drop ...', 'Approaching the edge ...', etc.).
   - The kind of information given first in most of the complex sentences.

4. Work on your own. Look at the way the text on page 58 ends. How does the way Step 6 is written help to ensure that the text appeals to the intended audience and achieve the writer's purpose?

Check! Work out a mnemonic or memory sentence that you can use to help you to remember the key features listed by your class that you should look for in a non-fiction text.

> Cliff jumping

Step 1 Work out text type, audience and purpose.

- What type of text is it?
  A mixture of instruction and explanation.
- Who is the intended audience?
  Less experienced skiers.
- What is the writer's purpose?
  To encourage the audience to try cliff jumping.

Step 2 Look out for the features on your checklist.

Search the text to see which of the features on your checklist the writer has used. When you find a feature, ask yourself how it suits the text's audience and purpose.

- font
- colour
- images
- headings
- introduction
- links
- sentence structure
- connectives
- verb tense and person
- conclusion
- choice of words

FREE RIDE>> CLIFF JUMP
THE THRILL AND FUN OF JUMPS IS ACCESSIBLE TO ALL – START WITH SOME POWDER AND A SMALL DROP, THEN USE THIS SIMPLE TAKE-OFF AND LANDING TECHNIQUE

Humongous cliff drops, often with a backflip thrown in, are now part and parcel of any big mountain freeride competition. And the extreme videos also feature many a plummeting plunge. This may all seem light years away from your average ski holiday, but that's just not the case – any advanced intermediate can enjoy the freeride buzz of dropping off small cliffs and rock bands, as long as you follow some simple guidelines to make sure you stay safe.

First, wait for a day of soft powder. You'll need at least a foot of freshies to soften up the landings sufficiently. Second, start small, and remember to avoid flat landings, as they create more damaging impact for your joints than if you land on a slope. Third, check both take-off and landing for rocks or branches hidden just below the snow. Finally, use a spotter to check the landing area is clear of other people before you drop in.

The cliff band in this sequence is a 15-footer in Vail's Back Bowls, but it's best to start with little two to three foot drops. The idea is to have fun, so don't scare yourself – and beware Kodak courage when your mate pulls out his point-and-press.

STEP 1
Skiing towards the drop, I prepare for flight by rooting both feet and poles securely to the ground – the four-point take-off position.

STEP 2
Approaching the edge, I use my knees to pull up my skis, feet and lower legs – often called the undercarriage – to avoid snagging my skis on the rocks of the cliff band when the snow begins to thin out.

STEPS 3 AND 4
During the drop I try to keep my hands forward in order to keep my position balanced and stable.

STEP 5
In anticipation of hitting the landing, I extend my legs, giving them the maximum potential to act as shock absorbers when the impact comes.

STEP 6
The secret to landing your jump is to be in the correct position for the depth and softness of where you're going to end up. The deeper the snow, the further back on your skis you'll need to be to avoid, in jumper's jargon, 'going over the handlebars'. It helps to watch others landing before your attempt. For stability, when I hit the ground I use the same four-point technique as I did when preparing for take-off.

Colour
Red – it's striking and picks out the key words 'cliff jump', making it look exciting, which suits the text's purpose. Grey – contrasts with the red. This grey looks soft – not threatening. It's used for the text that tries to make cliff jumping sound like something the reader can try.

Images
These pictures show readers how the jump is done step-by-step but you can't see the person's face. It could be anyone, even the audience, so maybe it helps readers picture themselves doing the jump, too? The jump looks as if it can be done – it's not too high. The clear blue sky and brilliant snow makes it look like a dream ski holiday – just what readers hope for. That will help make cliff jumping desirable to the reader.

> C2: Practice

The text below appeared in a skiing magazine and gives a mixture of instructions and explanations to readers so that they can learn how to jump off a cliff and land safely.

FREE RIDE>> CLIFF JUMP
THE THRILL AND FUN OF JUMPS IS ACCESSIBLE TO ALL – START WITH SOME POWDER AND A SMALL DROP, THEN USE THIS SIMPLE TAKE-OFF AND LANDING TECHNIQUE

➡ Humongous cliff drops, often with a backflip thrown in, are now part and parcel of any big mountain freeride competition. And the extreme videos also feature many a plummeting plunge. This may all seem light years away from your average ski holiday, but that's just not the case – any advanced intermediate can enjoy the freeride buzz of dropping off small cliffs and rock bands, as
5   long as you follow some simple guidelines to make sure you stay safe.

First, wait for a day of soft powder. You'll need at least a foot of freshies to soften up the landings sufficiently. Second, start small, and remember to avoid flat landings, as they create more damaging impact for your joints than if you land on a slope. Third, check both take-off and landing for rocks or branches hidden just below the snow. Finally, use a spotter to check the landing area is clear of other
10 people before you drop in.

The cliff band in this sequence is a 15-footer in Vail's Back Bowls, but it's best to start with little two to three foot drops. The idea is to have fun, so don't scare yourself – and beware Kodak courage when your mate pulls out his point-and-press.

STEP 1
15 Skiing towards the drop, I prepare for flight by rooting both feet and poles securely to the ground – the four-point take-off position.
STEP 2
Approaching the edge, I use my knees to pull up
20 my skis, feet and lower legs – often called the undercarriage – to avoid snagging my skis on the rocks of the cliff band when the snow begins to thin out.
STEPS 3 AND 4
25 During the drop I try to keep my hands forward in order to keep my position balanced and stable.

STEP 5
In anticipation of hitting the landing, I extend my legs, giving them the maximum potential to act as shock absorbers when the impact comes.   30
STEP 6
The secret to landing your jump is to be in the correct position for the depth and softness of where you're going to end up. The deeper the snow, the further back on your skis you'll need to   35 be to avoid, in jumper's jargon, 'going over the handlebars'. It helps to watch others landing before your attempt. For stability, when I hit the ground I use the same four-point technique as I did when preparing for take-off.   40

> From *Daily Mail Ski & Snowboard*, September 2002

58

> Cliff jumping

❓ HELP | Types of questions

The questions you are asked below focus on different types of reading skills.

- Question 1 requires you to select information from the text.
- Questions 2–3 require you to 'read between the lines'.
- Question 4 requires you to look at why the writer has structured and organised the text in a particular way.
- Questions 5–6 require you to investigate the writer's language choices.
- Question 7 requires you to look at the overall effect – how the writer's choices affect a reader's response.

↘ Questions

1 What is:
   a the 'four-point take-off position'? *(1 mark)*
   b the undercarriage? *(1 mark)*

2 Why does it help 'to watch others landing before your attempt' as suggested in Step 6? *(2 marks)*

3 Read the text that appears above the pictures. How has the writer made the idea of cliff jumping sound attractive to the audience? *(3 marks)*

4 How has the writer organised the text to make it easy for readers to follow the instructions? *(2 marks)*

5 What is the effect of writing the steps in the first person? *(2 marks)*

❓ HELP

When you answer question 5, think about the writer's audience and purpose. How does using the first person 'I' help the writer to get it right for this audience?

6 Why has the writer used:
   a dashes in Step 2? *(1 mark)*
   b inverted commas in the phrase 'going over the handlebars' in Step 6? *(1 mark)*

7 How has the writer made sure that this text suits its audience?
You should write about:
- who the audience is and how you can tell
- the way the text is presented
- the way reasons and explanations are given
- the type of language the writer uses. *(5 marks)*

> C2: Practice

? HELP

When you are answering a question like question 7, think carefully about what to write for each of the prompts given in the question. That way you will make sure that you cover all the points needed to get maximum marks for your answer. Keep asking yourself questions about the text to help you work out your ideas, for example:

Why did the writer use these colours for the heading?

Why did the writer use the words 'thrill' and 'fun'?

Why did the writer use the adjectives 'small' and 'simple'?

FREE RIDE>> CLIFF JUMP
THE THRILL AND FUN OF JUMPS IS ACCESSIBLE TO ALL – START WITH SOME POWDER AND A SMALL DROP, THEN USE THIS SIMPLE TAKE-OFF AND LANDING TECHNIQUE

So, I need to think about the heading. I need to work out: What is it about the heading that will grab the attention of new skiers?

Why does the writer want to tell this audience jumps are 'accessible to all'?

60

PRACTICE
C3 Snowboard

In this unit you will investigate how language is chosen to suit a particular audience.

KEY POINTS

Investigating how language is chosen for audience and purpose

In the test you may be asked to comment on how the writer's choice of language appeals to the target audience and achieves what the writer wants. As you know, first you need to work out what type of text you are reading, its audience and purpose (see page 8 for more help).

1. Work as a class. Read the *Amped* review on page 63. Discuss:
   a. What type of text is it? How can you tell?
   b. What sort of audience is it aimed at? How can you tell?
   c. What is the purpose of the text?

An expert writing for other experts can use technical terms, knowing that they will be understood. However, an expert writing for a wider audience needs to use simpler words and explain any technical term, to make sure everyone will understand the text.

2. When you are reading a text, notice the type of language the writer has used and work out how it suits the audience and purpose.
   Read the example opposite, which is taken from the *Amped* review, to help you do this. Remember, a writer might use more than one type of language in the same text.

3. Search through the text on page 63.
   a. Make a list of technical words that relate to **a)** snowboarding **b)** gaming.
   b. Decide whether each list of words or phrases is mostly used to inform, describe or give opinions. Give reasons for your decisions.

4. Now search through the text on page 63 again.
   a. Note down examples of informal language.
   b. Are these words or phrases used to inform, describe or give opinions? Give reasons for your answer.

5. Explore the persuasive qualities of the text.
   a. What sort of language has the writer used to persuade:
      • new gamers to try out *Amped*   • experienced players to buy *Amped*?
   b. Is the picture used in the review likely to persuade new gamers, experienced gamers, or both to play *Amped*? Give reasons for your answer.

Check! Work in pairs. Draw a flow chart showing how you can work out how a writer's choice of language suits a text's audience and purpose.

61

> C3: Practice

Step 1 Which different types of language are used?
For example formal, informal, emotive, technical, persuasive, colloquial (chatty), etc?

Step 2 Why does each of type of language suit the text's audience?
- Technical terms – the technical terms aren't explained, so the writer must expect the reader to understand them.
- Chatty phrases – these suit a teenage to early-twenties audience, who are the age group that buy and play Xbox games the most.

The controls are easy to master – three buttons grab your board and the B button grinds. The best tricks are big manoeuvres in which you swoosh your rider over an angled ramp, or natural ledge and spin him horizontally and vertically at once. Add a beautiful landing and you'll bag big points.

The **pro** challenges are particularly good. Shadowing a pro rider and attempting to beat their scores actually feels like learning to snowboard, both directly and indirectly. Beating him adds a new trick to the repertoire. Better still, observing the line he takes down the course exposes new areas, and teaches you how to exploit ramps and grind rails to the max.

Step 3 Why do the different types of language suit the text's purpose?
- Using technical terms makes the reviewer sound like an expert. Readers who already know a lot about games want to know that the writer knows a lot about the subject so they will trust the information he gives and his opinions if he uses a lot of jargon and technical terms correctly.
- The style is chatty and friendly – this makes readers feel like the writer is a fellow game player, telling them what is good and bad about the game. Readers are more likely to believe the opinion of a review written like this.

> Snowboard

The following review from a gaming magazine tells readers the pros and cons of an Xbox game called *Amped*.

AMPED: FREESTYLE SNOWBOARDING

You'll smash your legs, crack your skull and then come back for more. This is gaming addiction in its purest form.

This is a new type of extreme sports ⁵ thrill. *Amped* is all about taming the mountain, pulling off perfect big air tricks and developing a career as a world-class snowboarder. It's addictive, fun and looks Xboxing good too.

¹⁰ Your aim is simple enough – to become the best freestyle snowboarder on the planet. You'll get there by wowing sponsors and the media and by chaining together incredible moves on rails, jumps, ¹⁵ buildings and anything else you can see.

The controls are easy to master – three buttons grab your board and the B button grinds. The best tricks are big manoeuvres in which you swoosh your rider over an ²⁰ angled ramp or natural ledge and spin him horizontally and vertically at once. Add a beautiful landing and you'll bag big points.

The pro challenges are particularly good. Shadowing a pro rider and ²⁵ attempting to beat their scores actually feels like learning to snowboard, both directly and indirectly. Beating him adds a new trick to the repertoire. Better still, observing the line he takes down the course exposes new areas and teaches ³⁰ you how to exploit ramps and grind rails to the max.

AMPED'S ADDICTIVE, FUN AND LOOKS XBOXING GOOD TOO ³⁵

Amped gets tongue-chewingly tricky about half way up the world rankings. While frustration inevitably creeps in at this point, progression becomes a matter of honour. Sadly, there's no other single ⁴⁰ player game and the multiplayer game consists of up to four players taking turns to out trick each other, which is a very poor effort.

Despite the sticky moments, *Amped* ⁴⁵ successfully immerses you in a brilliantly believable Career. You really feel you're learning to ride each tricky mountain course and you're constantly rewarded with new levels, tricks, and kit along the ⁵⁰ way. It's a truly impressive game that will please gamers of all flavours. In fact it's, like, totally awesome.

> Adapted from *Xbox Gamer* magazine, March 2002

63

> C3: Practice

❓ HELP | Types of questions

The questions you are asked below focus on different types of reading skills.
- Questions 1 and 2 require you to select information from the text.
- Question 3 requires you to 'read between the lines'.
- Question 4 requires you to look at why the writer has structured and organised the text in a particular way.
- Question 5 requires you to investigate the writer's language choices.
- Question 6 requires you to look at the overall effect – how the writer's choices affect a reader's response.

↘ Questions

1   From paragraph 3, what do you have to do to become the best snowboarder while playing *Amped*?   **(1 mark)**

2   Find and list what the reviewer says are four of *Amped's* strengths and three of its weaknesses. Write your answers in a chart like the one below.

Strengths	Weaknesses
1	1
2	2
3	3
4	

(2 marks)

3   What kind of audience is this review aimed at? How can you tell?   **(2 marks)**

📗 REMEMBER | Targeting an audience

Writers of non-fiction grab their target audience's attention quickly. They make headings, pictures and the opening and closing paragraphs work for them. Always work out who the audience is by studying those features carefully. Ask yourself:
→ What kind of readers will this attract?
→ Why will it appeal to them particularly?

64

> Snowboard

4 Compare the headings and the bold print. Which is most effective at grabbing readers' attention? Why?

(2 marks)

HELP | Quoting evidence to support your answers

- When answering a question such as question 4, put yourself in the audience's shoes as you work out your answer. Give reasons for your decision.
- Refer to or quote from the text to prove that your view is sensible.
- Look at page 00 to remind yourself how to quote from a text.

5 Read the second and third paragraphs again. How does the writer's choice of adjectives (describing words) help to build a positive picture of the game?

(3 marks)

6 How does the writer try to convince readers that *Amped* is worth playing?
You should write about:
- how the writer has chosen language to suit the audience
- what information the writer gives about *Amped*
- how the writer describes playing *Amped*
- how and when the writer expresses his opinions.

(5 marks)

↘ Comparing texts

Read the explanation text on cliff jumping on page 58 and the review of *Amped* on page 63 carefully. Both are non-fiction texts. As well as similarities, there are some differences between them. Comment on three features of these texts that are different.

(3 marks)

HELP | Audience and purpose

In the test you may be asked to compare two texts that are linked in theme.

- In this unit, the texts you are asked to compare are both non-fiction. But are their target audiences and their purposes different?
- When you find text features that are different, comment on how well the feature suits the audience and purpose of each text. Support your comments with evidence.
- Explain why the different features chosen for each text are needed to suit each text's audience and purpose. Include comments on text presentation, use of language and vocabulary, and the variety of sentence structures used for different purposes.

PRACTICE
C4 Taken at face value

In this unit you will practise investigating how a theme is treated in fiction.

KEY POINTS

Recognising how writers present themes

1. a Which of the following could be a theme in a story?
   - Martin Turner
   - prejudice
   - Benjamin Zephaniah
   - faces
   - love
   - a nightclub
   - yesterday
   - a car crash

   b What is a theme?

   In the test you may be asked about the theme of a text. You need to be able to spot quickly what the theme is and work out what the writer is trying to show readers about it. Often a theme provides a problem for characters to face (such as being picked on because of the way they look) or causes conflict between characters (for example, they disagree because one character is prejudiced against someone and the other character is not). This means that looking carefully at the situations characters face, how they respond, how others treat them, and what is said and thought will help you to work out what the writer is trying to show readers.

2. Read the text on page 68. Then study the example opposite, which is taken from the text and shows how you can work out what the writer is trying to show you about a theme.

3. Now use the questions from the example on page 67 to help you make notes about what the writer is showing you about prejudice in these extracts from the text:
   a lines 13–19
   b lines 20–25.

4. Work in a group. Work out and perform a scene using the ingredients below to show what you think about prejudice.
   - Martin
   - A table in the school dinner hall
   - Characters who are prejudiced against people who look different
   - Characters who are not prejudiced against people who look different

5. Watch and talk about each other's scenes. What did they show you about prejudice? How did they show this?

Check! You have one minute to explain what questions will help you to work out the theme of a text and what the text shows about that theme.

Find a problem or conflict and ask the three questions below.

1 What is the reason for the conflict or problem?
The children won't leave Martin in peace.
They are horrible to him even though Martin has done nothing wrong.

2 Why are the characters behaving like this?
The children are treating Martin like this because of his face – he looks strange.
They are prejudiced.

> Some of the children jumped back and screamed. Others shouted abuse: 'Ugly man,' 'You're the bad man,' 'Dog face.' The kids shouted to each other, 'Don't let him touch you, he'll kill you,' 'If you look at him for long you'll go blind.' Some of them picked up twigs and pieces of paper from the ground and threw them at him, shouting, 'Get away, bogey man,' 'Here's your dinner,' 'You haven't got no Mommy or Daddy.'

3 What do the characters' words or behaviour show you about the theme?
(Make sure that you use the text to support your ideas.)
The children's cruel behaviour shows how awful prejudice is.
They don't try to find out what Martin is like or give him a chance.

> C4: Practice

Below is an extract from Benjamin Zephaniah's novel *Face*, which is about a teenager called Martin Turner whose face has been badly burned in a joyriding accident. Now he is out of hospital, Martin has to learn to deal with the way other people treat him because he looks so strange.

Face Value

At lunch time Martin decided to go for a walk in Plashet Park. He walked around the park until he came to a small area where there were swings, climbing frames and roundabouts. One of the roundabouts was empty. He pushed it, jumped on and then sat on the floor of it. He looked up into the sky and watched the clouds as he spun beneath them. Then he closed his eyes. He
5   was tired and for a moment he let his mind drift. The roundabout stopped but he kept his eyes shut until he was disturbed by whispers. He opened his eyes to find that he was surrounded by a group of about ten children, none of them older than eleven.

Some of the children jumped back and screamed. Others shouted abuse: 'Ugly man,' 'You're the bad man,' 'Dog face.' The kids shouted to each other, 'Don't let him touch you, he'll kill you,' 'If you look
10   at him for long you'll go blind.' Some of them picked up twigs and pieces of paper from the ground and threw them at him, shouting, 'Get away, bogey man,' 'Here's your dinner,' 'You haven't got no Mommy or Daddy.'

There were so many of them. It was happening so quickly that Martin was speechless. He stood up and the kids backed off but they stayed close enough to carry on shouting their nasty words.
15   He shouted, 'Go away, will you,' but they got even more noisy and began to follow him. He turned around and ran towards them but they screamed louder and ran off in various directions before regrouping. He tried chasing them a second time and they scattered again. It was useless. *Which one shall I run after*? he thought. *What do I do once I catch one of them*? he thought. He gave up but the children didn't, they trailed behind him again.
20   Then he heard a woman's far off voice. 'Get away, you lot! What are you doing? Leave him alone!'

The children all turned around and ran off. Martin didn't look where they went, nor did he hang around to speak to the woman; he was too upset and he didn't want any pity. He just carried on walking home with his head hung low, depressed and disheartened. It was the worst
25   he had felt for ages. After all that he had survived on the streets and at school, it took a group of ten year olds to send him to an all time low, he thought. He didn't know how to argue with a group of that age. He couldn't fight a group of that age. They seemed to hate him, they thought he was evil, they were purposely cruel. Their images and words stayed with him as he walked home. At the top of Plashet Grove he turned right and began to walk down the High Street. He
30   felt as if everyone's eyes were on him.

> From *Face* by Benjamin Zephaniah

> Taken at face value

HELP | Types of questions

The questions you are asked below focus on different types of reading skills.

- Question 1 requires you to select information from the text.
- Question 2 requires you to 'read between the lines'.
- Question 3 requires you to look at why the writer has structured and organised the text in a particular way.
- Question 4 requires you to investigate the writer's language choices.
- Question 5 requires you to look at the overall effect – how the writer's choices affect a reader's response.

Questions

1 From the text, decide whether the following statements are true or false.
   a Martin has fallen asleep on a roundabout when he is attacked.
   b Martin's attackers are aged ten and under and there are eleven of them.
   c The children throw sticks and paper at Martin.
   d Martin chases the children but doesn't catch them.
   e A man with a dog walks past and does nothing.
   f Martin feels grateful and relieved after the woman rescues him. *(3 marks)*

2 In the second paragraph, read what the children shout at Martin. What do their insults tell you about the way the children view people whose faces are different from their own? *(2 marks)*

3 In what ways do the first and second paragraphs contrast with each other? *(2 marks)*

HELP | Looking for contrasts

When you are looking for contrasts between two paragraphs in a story, look for the different events, people, moods or feelings described and notice the way they are written about. Study the sentences and vocabulary and ask yourself questions about them, for example:

- Are the sentences short simple statements or long, complex descriptions?
- Is the vocabulary emotive or persuasive, dialogue or narrative?

When you notice a difference in the way different things are written about, look at each one in turn and ask yourself:

- Why does this sort of writing suit what is being described?

> C4: Practice

4. In paragraphs 4 and 5, read what Martin and the woman say to the children.
   a Who is more confident when speaking to them? *(1 mark)*
   b How does the way that person's dialogue is written show confidence? *(1 mark)*

5. What does the text show you about the theme of prejudice?
   You should write about:
   - why Martin is attacked
   - how different characters respond to Martin's situation
   - the way the text is presented
   - how readers are encouraged to empathise with Martin
   - the way Martin's feelings change during this extract
   - the writer's use of language. *(5 marks)*

❓ HELP | The way the text is presented

In the test you may be asked to consider 'the way the text is presented' in fiction. Although fiction writers often do not use all the same presentational features as non-fiction writers (such as headings or pictures), they might use different prints such as italics, bold print, capital letters or underlining. When you find examples of these in the text, work out why those words are emphasised using the following three questions.

1. **What sorts of words or ideas are emphasised in this way?**
   a The children's insults – what sort of things they say.
   b Martin's thoughts – about the people who are abusing him and what he should do.

2. **Why are the emphasised things important in the story?**
   a The children's insults are the way they show their prejudice. Some of the insults are accusations – 'You're the bad man'. Others are descriptions – 'Dog face'. Others are warnings – 'If you look at him for long you'll go blind'. All of the insults are lies.
   b Martin's thoughts show how difficult it is to know what to do when someone treats you badly. He is unsure of what to do and questions his behaviour saying: 'What do I do once I catch one of them?'

3. **What does emphasising these things make readers notice?**
   The horrible way prejudiced people behave – prejudice is childish behaviour. Martin is a teenager and he questions how he should deal with the children's prejudice. The adult woman is not prejudiced and she challenges the children by saying: 'What are you doing?' She stops them behaving in a prejudiced way, telling them: 'Get away, you lot' and 'Leave him alone!'

PRACTICE
C5 Working angels

In this unit you will practise investigating a persuasive text.

KEY POINTS

Recognising how texts persuade

1. a Split into teams. Follow the instructions below and play Auction. The first team to reach £100 wins.
   b List the different ways in which people tried to persuade bidders.

Auction

Speakers
One person in each team is chosen as the speaker. As the speaker, choose an item in the room, such as a chair, table, pencil case. You have one minute to persuade people in your class to bid for it. Be as imaginative and persuasive as you like, for example:
What am I bid for this fine example of an antique chair? It is said that the Queen of England once …

Listeners
As you listen, note the different things that are said to persuade you (for example: (1) it's an antique; (2) it was used by the Queen, etc.). Each persuasive thing you note gives you £1 to bid with once the speaker has finished.

Bidding
When the speaker has finished, the person who has noted down the highest number of persuasive comments wins the bid for the item and the same number of points for their team.

In the test you may be asked to explain how the writer has persuaded readers. It will help you to bear in mind that to persuade readers a writer has to:
- make them believe that what the writer wants them to do is a good idea
- overcome any objections readers might have.

This is why you need to study the choices that the writer makes about:
- form (a personal letter, a leaflet, an advertisement, etc.)
- layout and presentation (which pictures to use, what to put in bold print, etc.)
- details (selecting what to include and what to leave out)
- what facts to give (for example, facts that will agree with the point the writer wants to make)
- what opinions to express (for example, including strong opinions that favour the writer's viewpoint)
- how to describe people, places and things (to arouse certain emotions in readers)
- how to overcome possible objections (for example by anticipating what readers might object to and having a good answer to them).

71

> C5: Practice

2 Read the letter on pages 73–74. Then study the example below, which is the opening paragraph of the letter. What should you look for to find out how a writer persuades readers?

Step 1 Read the whole text and ask yourself the following questions.
- **What does the writer want readers to do?**
  Give money to a charity called Ethiopiaid so that they can support the work of the House of Angels.
- **Who is the audience?**
  People who already support Ethiopiaid.
- **What feeling does it appeal to?**
  People's feelings of pity and kindness.

> **I was shocked and humbled by what I saw at the House of Angels**
> **Please, let me tell you why**
>
> Dear Supporter
>
> I feel compelled to tell you about the amazing work of the nuns who run a hospital we call the House of Angels, a centre for the sick and dying in Ethiopia's capital city, Addis Ababa.

Step 2 Study the heading, each paragraph and picture in turn, looking at the details carefully. Work out how the writer is trying to persuade readers by asking yourself three questions. An examination of the heading has been done for you as an example.
- **What does it mean?**
  The writer has been deeply moved by a place called the House of Angels and wants to tell readers why.
- **What does it suggest?**
  It suggests that what the writer has to say is important.
- **Why will it persuade readers?**
  These words touch readers' feelings (they are **emotive** words).
  Something terrible like this will shock people and make them feel pity, but angels are good and kind – readers wonder what the letter is all be about and want to read on.
  It's very polite – readers like being treated respectfully.

3
- a Work in groups. Spend ten minutes searching the letter for all the different persuasive techniques used by the writer.
- b Then use the questions in the example above to help you to work out how and why each technique on your list works in this letter.
- c Share and compare your findings with the rest of the class.

Check! Draw a mind map to help you to remember the different persuasive techniques that writers might use and how to investigate them.

> Working angels

Below is a letter sent by a charity called Ethiopiaid. The letter is addressed to people who have already given money once and asks them for further help.

ETHIOPIAID

PO Box 31052 London SW1X 9WB
(office space kindly donated)
Tel: 01753 868277 Fax: 01753 841688
e-mail: ethiopiaid@reed.co.uk Internet: www.ethiopiaid.org.uk
Registered Charity No: 802353

HELP THE POOREST PEOPLE ON EARTH

R Thomson   78700
15 Maple Avenue
Milton Keynes
Buckinghamshire
MK13 2TY

W0502b/M1049523
00014530

May 2002

I was shocked and humbled by what I saw at the House of Angels
Please, let me tell you why

Dear Supporter

I feel compelled to tell you about the amazing work of the nuns who run a hospital we call the House of Angels, a centre for the sick and dying in Ethiopia's capital city, Addis Ababa. I am shocked by the sheer poverty and desperation of the patients, but also deeply humbled by the absolute
5   dedication of the nuns who care for them.

The sick make their way to the hospital gates, often with the help of friends, family or even kind strangers. Some already live on the streets of Addis Ababa but others have travelled many hundreds of miles from the countryside to seek help. On a recent visit, I saw a woman with her baby
10 lying on the road outside the gates, too weak to move any closer, but thankful that they would soon be carried inside.

Ethiopiaid struggles hard to focus on the goal of long-term self-sufficiency, <u>but this is one project that we cannot turn our backs on</u>. The immediate relief that the nuns provide is absolutely essential to the men,
15 women and children who flood through their doors every single day. Currently over 750 people are admitted each month, suffering from illnesses such as tuberculosis, malnutrition and the ravages of AIDS. These people have no money to pay for their treatment and, without the House of Angels, would have nowhere to turn.

20 We have no photos taken inside the hospital. If you visited this place you would agree that it would be entirely inappropriate. Every room is kept spotlessly clean, despite the reality of vomit and uncontrolled defecation. <u>Although many of the patients do not survive, they are able to pass away with a dignity not afforded to them on the streets.</u>

continued overleaf

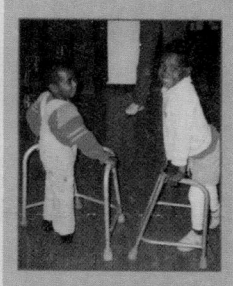

> C5: Practice

25 The nuns who work devotedly as nurses never cease to amaze me. They work every day for five years before taking a month's rest. One of them, Annie, told me how her motivation came from a deep religious devotion to help the destitute. She does not want our sympathy or even our praise for her work. **But she does need your donation to continue caring for**
30 **the sick and the dying**.

In a second building lie tiny cots. From each cot, two dark eyes peer out – all belong to children orphaned shortly after birth. Some are sad and pathetic but others are hopeful, full of a child's endless optimism and expectation of love.

35 I met two children at the orphanage who had been picked up from the streets just that day. A girl of about six and her little brother, both so lost and terrified that they were unable to look at me. No one had any idea what had become of their parents. The nuns were waiting for the results of the children's HIV tests. Hopefully they will be negative and the
40 children will be eligible for adoption.

If not, they will go to another home, one solely for children with HIV/AIDS. Sadly, most of the two hundred children I met there are unlikely to reach their teenage years. Yet the happy smiles on their faces are testament to the nuns who care for them. They are just a handful of
45 the one million children in Ethiopia who have been orphaned by AIDS.

The nuns I met at the House of Angels have given their lives to these people, the poorest of the poor. Some days even they must have their doubts in the face of such misery. But the donations we hope to send out next month will remind them that there are still many individuals in the
50 west who are sensitive to the suffering of their distant neighbours.

These amazing women have a love for people and a passion for their vocation that humbles me. They do, however, need the financial support of people like you and me to enable them to ease the lives of more desperate Ethiopians and to let those they cannot save die with dignity in
55 a place of peace and respect.

On their behalf,
Yours sincerely

Alec Reed

Voluntary Chairman of Trustees

60 P.S. I doubt I would have the courage to work alongside the nuns at the House of Angels. But at least I know that I can support them financially. You can also help by sending a donation today.

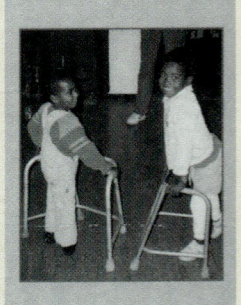

> Ethiopiaid

> Working angels

❓ HELP | Types of questions

The questions you are asked below focus on different types of reading skills.
- Question 1 requires you to select information from the text.
- Question 2 requires you to 'read between the lines'.
- Question 3 requires you to look at why the writer has structured and organised the text in a particular way.
- Question 4 requires you to investigate the writer's language choices.
- Question 5 requires you to look at the overall effect – how the writer's choices affect a reader's response.

↘ Questions

1. Copy and complete the chart below with three pieces of information you are told about:
   a the nuns who work at the House of Angels
   b the different groups of people helped by the nuns.

Information about the nuns	Different groups of people helped by the nuns
1	1
2	2
3	3

(2 marks)

2. Why is it important for the writer to explain the two points below to readers?

   a
   > Ethiopiaid struggles hard to focus on the goal of long-term self-sufficiency, but this is one project that we cannot turn our backs on. The immediate relief that the nuns provide is absolutely essential to the men, women and children who flood through their doors every single day. (lines 12–15)

   (2 marks)

   b
   > We have no photos taken inside the hospital. If you visited this place you would agree that it would be entirely inappropriate. (lines 20–21)

   (2 marks)

75

> C5: Practice

❓ HELP | How texts persuade readers

Writers of persuasive texts have to overcome any reasons readers might have for not doing what the writer wants them to and gain trust of their readers. In the quotations in question 2, the writer addresses reasons why readers may not be sure about sending Ethiopiaid money to help this project. Try to work out what the reasons might be.

3   Find each of the following presentational features in the text and explain why it has been used:
    a   bold print *(1 mark)*
    b   underlined text *(1 mark)*
    c   handwriting font. *(1 mark)*

❗ REMEMBER

In the test you won't earn marks by just saying that bold print is used to emphasise something. You need to explain:
→   what is being emphasised
→   why it is important for readers to notice that information.

4   Explain the impact on readers' feelings of the underlined words in the following quotation.

> The nuns I met at the House of Angels have given their lives to these people, <u>the poorest of the poor</u>. Some days <u>even they</u> must have their doubts <u>in the face of such misery</u>. (lines 46–48)

(3 marks)

5   Explain how the writer persuades readers to give their money to this charity.
    You should write about:
    ● the writer's choice of form – a personal letter
    ● the way the letter is presented
    ● what readers are told about the nuns and the needy people
    ● the impression of Ethiopiaid that is created
    ● the writer's choice of language
    ● the variety of sentence structures used. *(5 marks)*

↘ Comparing texts

The writers of the extract 'Face value' on page 68 and the Ethiopiaid letter on pages 73–74 both try to stir up readers' feelings. Compare the ways in which they do this.
You should write about:
● the different situations described
● how readers' feelings are roused
● the way language is used. *(3 marks)*

PRACTICE
C6 Different worlds?

In this unit you will practise investigating the way a web text targets its audience.

KEY POINTS

Recognising the way web texts target their audience

1. Read the text on page 79. Brainstorm a list of the different features you might find on a web page.

Website readers will scan a web page as it arrives on screen and decide in a matter of seconds whether to stay on the site and read the text or move on. This means that first impressions are vital, so a web page writer has to make sure that the appearance of the text grabs the attention of the audience immediately.

Writers also know that readers will only stay on a site, revisit it or tell others about it if the content and design make the pages interesting and straightforward to use. Since most readers will be skimming the text for information rather than reading it in depth, it is important that any prose is written in a way that makes it easy to understand quickly.

2. Read the example on page 78 which is taken from a web text, and find out how to investigate the way a web text targets its audience.

3. Work in a group. Read the whole web page on page 79 again. Use the questions on page 78 to help you look at the text. Discuss the ways in which the writer has tried to make sure that readers will revisit the site or tell others about it.

4. Work in a group. Look at the layout of the web page below. How would you change the position of different features to target the audience better? Give reasons for your changes.

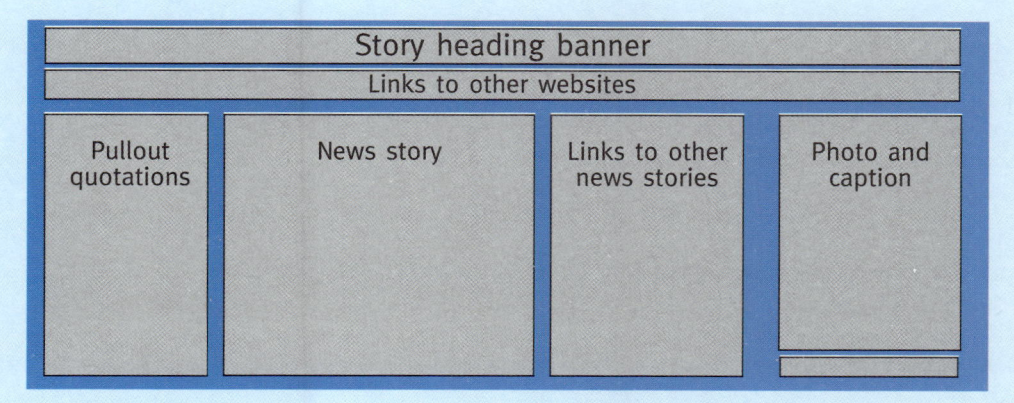

Story heading banner			
Links to other websites			
Pullout quotations	News story	Links to other news stories	Photo and caption

Check! Speak for a minute on how web page writers target audiences.

> C6: Practice

Step 1 How does the text instantly grab the readers' attention?
By using colour, headings and a colour photo, with people in it.

Step 2
a What impression of the site does the layout create? How does it achieve this?
It looks serious and trustworthy. It achieves this by using plain colours like brown, grey and black and by being informative not chatty or persuasive.
b Why is this an important message to readers?
The BBC wants to be taken seriously.

Step 3 How has the writer made sure that the audience will read the main text?
The heading, picture and caption give the gist of the story. The short paragraphs make the text easy to read.

Charity calls for 'net-free' day

Net users told 'leave the virtual world – try the real one'

Computer users are being urged to take a break from the screen this Sunday by an internet-based charity which is calling for a worldwide net-free day.

The idea behind the second International Internet-Free Day is to persuade people to leave their PCs at home and get out into the 'real world'.

Ironically, the call is being made by an internet-based group, Do Be, which provides free bulletin boards where people can propose events, groups and meetings for others to sign up for.

Step 4 Think about the whole website. How does the writer show readers what else it offers?
By:
- *making links to other web pages*
- *listing titles of other stories that may interest readers*
- *choosing words in headings to attract attention and hook readers, such as 'Top UK stories'.*

Step 5 How has the writer made it easy for readers to scan and skim the text quickly?
By using:
- *headings in colour*
- *columns to separate different types of information*
- *large, clear font*
- *short lines of text*
- *single sentence paragraphs*
- *a concise style.*

> **Different worlds**

The news report below from the BBC website informs readers about a charity event that could change their world – for a day.

UK NEWS

Saturday, 26 January, 2002, 13:01 GMT

Charity calls for 'net-free' day

Top UK Stories:
- Blair calls for war
- House prices continue to rise
- Postcode lottery in GP services

- World
- UK
- Local
- UK Government
- City and finance
- Entertainment
- Sport
- Your views

Net users told 'leave the virtual world – try the real one'

See also:
- 20 Jul 01 | Asia-Pacific — Japan assists web 'addicts'
- 08 Apr 00 | Middle East — Internet addiction strikes Iraq
- 16 Aug 99 | Sci/Tech — What makes the web tick?

Internet links:
- Do Be
- Friends Reunited

> It's about creating a balance between the web and the real world
> – Stephanie Wienrich, Promoter, Net-Free Day

Computer users are being urged to take a break from the screen this Sunday by an internet-based charity which is calling for a worldwide net-free day.

The idea behind the second International Internet-Free Day is to persuade people to leave their PCs at home and get out into the 'real world'.

Ironically, the call is being made by an internet-based group, Do Be, which provides free bulletin boards where people can propose events, groups and meetings for others to sign up for.

Do Be wants individuals or organisations to arrange events where 'participants can make a real contribution, feel recognised as unique individuals and perhaps form friendships with others who share their interests'.

Launched in September 2000, the non-profit website DoBe.org carries listings for more than 10,000 cities all over the world.

'Turn it off'

Stephanie Wienrich, a spokeswoman for Do Be's London site, told BBC Radio 4's *Today* programme: 'We are basically trying to persuade people for just one day to do something, anything, that involves the real world – either meeting people, walking, cycling or just getting out. We are going for a river walk on the South Bank in London.'

She adds: 'By all means use e-mail and the web to prearrange to meet up with people – but do turn it off on the day itself.'

Ms Wienrich said there had been a definite culture change with younger people being more inclined to stay at home.

She said: 'I don't know if you can solely blame the internet for that but it is definitely a factor in it. We are just asking people to think about creating more of a balance between the web and real world activities.'

Addictive

Steve Pankhurst, one of the founders of Friends Reunited, which is now among the UK's biggest websites, was not convinced people would switch off.

He said: 'I think we would get too many complaints from our members if we switched off.'

But he added: 'I do think there are certain areas of the internet, like chatrooms, that are addictive to certain people in the same way that television is to some. But there is a place for everything, and if you use the internet correctly, and use it for information, I don't see a problem.'

> From BBC News Online

> C6: Practice

HELP | Types of questions

The questions you are asked below focus on different types of reading skills.
- Question 1 requires you to select information from the text.
- Question 2 requires you to 'read between the lines'.
- Questions 3 and 4 require you to look at why the writer has structured and organised the text in a particular way.
- Question 5 requires you to look at the overall effect – how the writer's choices affect a reader's response.

Questions

1. Give four activities that people could do on International Internet-Free Day instead of sitting at their computers. *(2 marks)*

2. What do the words 'real world' in paragraphs 2 and 6 suggest about time spent using the Internet? *(2 marks)*

3. Explain how beginning the news story with the picture and caption directly under the heading helps to hook readers. *(3 marks)*

HELP

When answering question 3, think about how much of the text can be seen on screen at any one time, and how quickly readers decide whether to stay on that web page or move on.

4. Explain how using single sentence paragraphs helps the writer to target the audience effectively. *(2 marks)*

5. How has the writer of this web page encouraged readers to make more use of the BBC website?
   You should write about:
   - the presentational features used
   - different ways readers are encouraged to interact with this web page
   - how the news article grabs readers' attention
   - the type of language the writer has used. *(5 marks)*

REMEMBER

You will earn more marks in the test if you support your answers by:
→ referring to or briefly quoting from relevant parts of the text
→ explaining how the part of the text you refer to proves your point.

> Different worlds

↘ Comparing texts

Read the Ethiopiaid letter on pages 73–74 and the BBC web page on page 79 carefully. Both these texts are carefully crafted to target their audiences. As well as similarities, there are some differences in the way they do this. Comment on three different ways these texts target their audiences.

(3 marks)

❓ HELP | How writers reach their audience

In the test you may be asked to compare the way two texts target their audiences. Below is a guide you can use to answer this kind of question.

Step 1 Ask yourself some questions about the audience for each text.
- Who is the audience?
- How will the audience read the text?
- Why will the audience want to read the text?

Step 2 Work out the purpose of each text.
- What does the writer want the reader to do?
- What impression of the product or issue does the writer want to give?

Step 3 Look at the way the text is written to suit its audience.
- What are the features of presentation?
- Is the content suitable for the intended audience?

❗ REMEMBER

If a text is written for different audiences, or is intended to be read in different ways, or for different purposes, the writer has to match the way the text is written to those readers so that it achieves its purpose.

PRACTICE
C7 Tiger!

In this unit you will practise responding to the sort of descriptions you are likely to meet in fiction or literary non-fiction.

KEY POINTS

Responding to a description

1. Work in pairs. Take it in turns to think of an animal that is scary and describe it to your partner as vividly as you can. Include things such as the animal's colour, shape, etc. Then:
   a. make a list of the different features you mentioned in your description
   b. underline anything that you exaggerated to make the animal scarier.

2. Read the text on page 84, on which you will be answering questions later. Discuss how you would investigate the way the writer made the tiger fearsome.

In the test you are likely to be asked questions about the way writer has built up a description. You need to be able to discover quickly what the writer has done. Working through the following four steps will help you.

Step 1 Search the description for details.
These will give you clues about what impression the writer is creating.

Step 2 Study each detail you find and ask:
- What do these words mean?
- What impression do these words create?

Step 3 Find other details that help to build up the same picture or feeling.

Step 4 Notice whether anything is exaggerated.
This is one way the writer can make an impression more powerful.

3. Now read the example opposite, which is taken from the text and shows how a reader used this guide to look closely at the details used in the first 4 lines of the text on page 84.

> Tiger!

Step 1 Search the description for details that give you clues about what impression the writer is creating.

Step 2 Study each detail you find and ask:
What does this mean?
The tiger's breath and fur smell horrible.
What do these words suggest?
It is dirty and hot, it's a wild animal not a pet – perhaps it is sweating.

The tiger padded through the night. Joe Maloney smelt it, the hot, sour breath, the stench of its pelt. The odour crept through the streets, through his open window and into his dreams. He felt the animal wildness on his tongue, in his nostrils. The tiger moved as if it knew him, as if it was drawn to him. Joe heard its footpads on the stairs.

Step 3 Find other details that help to build up the same picture or feeling.
These sentences make the animal seem wild and frightening. The words 'crept ... through ... into' make the movement seem threatening. The word 'wildness' reinforces the idea that this animal isn't tame – it still smells of the jungle.

Step 4 Notice whether anything is exaggerated.
The movement of the smell is exaggerated to make it seem like a wild animal creeping up on Joe. Then when the tiger really does come towards him it's even scarier because you know that if the smell can reach him so can the tiger!

4 Now it is your turn to use the same four steps to help you to search different parts of the text on page 84 carefully and work out what the details are suggesting. You can note your ideas in a chart like the one below.

Lines	Details	What it means	What it suggests
3–5	1 'footpads on the stairs' 2	The tiger is in the house	It's coming to get him – this is scary
6–8			
9–23			

5 Talk as a class about which details in the text work together to:
   a make the tiger scary
   b make you think that Joe is in danger.

Check! Work in pairs. Close your books. Then take it in turns to explain how to go about searching a description and responding to its details.

83

> C7: Practice

The following extract is the introduction to David Almond's novel *Secret Heart*. It describes a disturbing dream that the main character, Joe Maloney, experiences.

TIGER!

The tiger padded through the night. Joe Maloney smelt it, the hot, sour breath, the stench of its **pelt**. The odour crept through the streets, through his open window and into his dreams. He felt the animal wildness on his tongue, in his nostrils. The tiger moved as if it knew him, as if it was drawn to him. Joe heard its footpads on the stairs.
5 He heard its long slow breath, the distant sighing in its lungs, the rattle in its throat. It came inside. It filled the bedroom. The huge head hung over him. The glittering cruel eyes stared into him. The hot tongue, harsh as sandpaper, licked his arm. The mouth was wide open, the curved teeth were poised to close on him. He prepared to die. Then someone somewhere called:
10 'Tiger! Tiger! Tiger! Tiger!'
And it was gone.
At the window he made a funnel of his hands and peered out. There it was, loping away
15 beneath the orange streetlights on the pale pavement between the pale houses. Longer than a man, taller than a boy. 'Tiger!' he gasped, and it paused and
20 swung its head to search him out. 'Tiger!' he whispered, as its eyes steadied and it gazed up at him.
'Tiger!' someone called, and
25 he saw the man – a huge dark figure in the shadows of the Cut. 'Tiger!'
Before it turned again, the tiger watched the boy. Stars
30 glittered in its eyes. It drew Joe Maloney into itself. Then it turned again and loped on towards the Cut. Hips and shoulders rocked. Tail swung. It
35 returned to the dark figure waiting there, and they left his sight, left the village, went into the deeper night outside.

> From *Secret Heart* by David Almond

Word bank

pelt – the skin and fur of an animal

> Tiger!

❓ HELP | Types of questions

Before you answer the questions below, read them through and work out which requires you to:
- select information from the text
- 'read between the lines'
- look at why the writer has structured and organised the text in a particular way
- investigate the writer's language choices
- look at the overall effect – how the writer's choices affect a reader's response.

↘ Questions

1. Read lines 12–23 and write down:
   a two facts you are told about the tiger *(1 mark)*
   b two facts you are told about the man who calls to the tiger. *(1 mark)*

2. What do the sentences below suggest about Joe and the tiger?
   a
   > The tiger moved as if it knew him, as if it was drawn to him. (lines 3–4)

   (1 mark)

   b
   > 'Tiger!' he gasped, and it paused and swung its head to search him out. 'Tiger!' he whispered, as its eyes steadied and it gazed up at him. (lines 18–23)

   (1 mark)

❓ HELP | Investigating key words

When you need to work out what a sentence suggests, pick out the key words.
Then think about each of those words in turn while asking yourself these questions.
- What does it mean?
- What does it suggest?

3. In lines 1–9 some sentences are short and some sentences are long. What effect is created by using different sentence lengths? *(2 marks)*

❗ REMEMBER | Different sentence lengths

→ Short sentences often just tell the reader what happened. Since there are no extra details the action has more impact on the reader.
→ Groups of short sentences build pace and can create tension.
→ Longer sentences allow the writer to include more detail and the pace feels slower and more relaxed.

85

> C7: Practice

4 Explain the effect of the describing words in each of these sentences from the text.

a
> Joe Maloney smelt it, the hot, sour breath, the stench of its pelt. (lines 1–2)

(1 mark)

b
> He heard its long slow breath, the distant sighing in its lungs, the rattle in its throat. (line 5)

(1 mark)

c
> The huge head hung over him. The glittering cruel eyes stared into him. The hot tongue, harsh as sandpaper, licked his arm. (lines 6–7)

(1 mark)

5 This extract is the opening of a novel. Explain how it grabs the reader's attention and makes them want to read on.
You should write about:
- what happens
- the way tension is built up in the first paragraph
- the way the tiger is described
- the relationship between Joe and the tiger
- any questions the reader might have after reading the opening. *(5 marks)*

HELP

When you are answering the longer questions in the test:
- begin a new paragraph each time you write about a new prompt
- remember to make a point, prove it by quoting or referring to the text and then explain how that example from the text proves your point
- keep referring to what the question is asking for.

Use the following sentence starters, phrases and connectives to help you to write your answer.

The passage starts with … This hooks readers because …

Tension builds in the first paragraph because the writer has … such as … This makes readers want to read on because …

The writer describes the tiger as … The writer creates this impression by using the words … which suggest …

After reading the opening readers will still be wondering …

PRACTICE
C8 Things that go scrunch in the night

In this unit you will practise investigating how suspense is created.

KEY POINTS

Recognising how suspense is created

1 Read the text on page 89. Work as a class and decide:
   a What is suspense?
   b Which of these ingredients could you use to build suspense?
   - something getting further and further away
   - something creeping up on someone
   - being with a big friendly group of people
   - the thing getting nearer and nearer
   - strange noises
   - seeing something move but not knowing what it is
   - being attacked by an eagle
   - being on your own
   c In what order would you use the ingredients you chose?

When we are waiting for something nasty to happen we have a feeling of suspense. A writer can encourage readers to experience suspense by:
- picking out only scary or threatening details to tell readers
- dropping hints that something nasty is going to happen
- telling readers what happens little by little
- keeping what happens a secret till the end.

Of course, how the suspense ends depends on what kind of a story the writer is telling. If something awful happens then it is a horror story, but if something unexpected and funny happens then the suspense has a different effect. The effect is like a good joke where you wait for the punch line.

2 Read the two steps and the annotated examples on page 88, which are taken from the text on page 89, and find out how to spot the way suspense is built up in a text and how the suspense is used to improve the ending.

> C8: Practice

Step 1 Search for the first hint that something strange is happening.
At this stage the sound is only 'curious' and 'fairly loud' and 'scrunching', which isn't too scary.

> I heard a curious sound that seemed to emanate from the forest behind our little hut. It was a fairly loud scrunching noise ... (lines 1–2)

Step 2 Search for the next hint. Then work out how it builds up the suspense.
The suspense grows because the noise is stronger, closer and coming at the writer from different directions.

> ... I was startled by the rasping matchbox noise again, this time very much closer and from several different directions. (lines 15–16)

3   In what order would you use the following quotations from the text to build up suspense? Explain how putting them in your order would build up suspense.
   a   'What the hell can it be?' asked John.
   b   I shone my torch at the banana-leaf roof and saw it was quivering and swaying, as though in an earthquake.
   c   ... the walls and the roof of the hut started to vibrate.
   d   Just then, there was a positive battery of rasping noises ...
   e   John, who had woken up, sat up and stared at me.
       'What's that?' he enquired, sleepily.

4   Check your ideas against what the writer did by reading up to line 31 on page 89. How does the way he wrote it build up tension?

5   Read the last paragraph and find out how the tension ends. What kind of story is this?

6   Look back through the earlier part of the story. Are there any hints that the ending is going to be humorous?

Check!   Make a poster to help you remember how to spot the way suspense is built up in a text.

Things that go scrunch in the night

I heard a curious sound that seemed to emanate from the forest behind our little hut. It was a fairly loud scrunching noise. It sounded to me, for some bizarre reason, like a matchbox being crushed in the hands of a very powerful man. Reluctantly I was forced to admit that, eccentric though the Rodriguans might be, it was unlikely that they crept about rain-drenched forests at three in the morning crushing matchboxes. Taking a torch, I eased my way out of our fragile hut and went to investigate. This was not quite so intrepid as it may appear, since there is nothing harmful in the animal line in Rodrigues, if you ignore the human animal. I made a careful search of the forest behind the hut, but could find nothing living that looked as though its normal cry resembled the crushing of a matchbox, and met nothing more ferocious than a large moth which seemed intent on trying to fly up the barrel of my torch. I went back to the hut and sat there, thinking. I wondered if we would catch any bats in the morning. Time was running short and I was debating with myself whether to move the nets nearer to the colony's roosting site. As I was pondering this problem, I was startled by the rasping matchbox noise again, this time very much closer and from several different directions. John, who had woken up, sat up and stared at me.

'What's that?' he enquired, sleepily.

'I haven't the faintest idea, but it's been going on for about ten minutes. I had a look round and I couldn't see anything.'

Just then, there was a positive battery of rasping noises, and the walls and the roof of the hut started to vibrate.

'What the hell can it be?' asked John.

I shone my torch at the banana-leaf roof and saw it was quivering and swaying, as though in an earthquake. Before we could do anything intelligent, the whole roof gave way and a cascade of giant landsnails, each the size of a small apple, descended upon us. They were fat, glossy and wet, and they gleamed in the torchlight, frothing gently and leaving an interesting pattern of slime on our beds. It took us ten minutes to rid our shelter of these unwanted gastropods and to repair the roof.

> From *Golden Bats and Pine Pigeons* by Gerald Durrell

> C8: Practice

> **HELP | Types of questions**
>
> Before you answer the questions below, read them through and work out which requires you to:
> - select information from the text
> - 'read between the lines'
> - look at why the writer has structured and organised the text in a particular way
> - investigate the writer's language choices
> - look at the overall effect – how the writer's choices affect a reader's response.

Questions

1. In what order do the following pieces of information appear in the text?
   a Giant landsnails are the size of apples.
   b Giant landsnails leave slimy trails.
   c Giant landsnails make a scrunching noise as they move.
   d Giant landsnails can climb on to high surfaces. *(1 mark)*

2. What does Gerald Durrell suggest by the underlined text? (lines 6–8)

   > Taking a torch, I eased my way out of our fragile hut and went to investigate. <u>This was not quite so intrepid as it may appear</u>, since there is nothing harmful in the animal line in Rodrigues, <u>if you ignore the human animal</u>.

   (2 marks)

3. Read the sentence below (lines 32–36). How does the order of the clauses add to the suspense?

   > Before we could do anything intelligent, the whole roof gave way and a cascade of giant landsnails, each the size of a small apple, descended upon us.

   (2 marks)

> Things that go scrunch in the night

❓ HELP | The order of clauses

If you are not sure what effect the order of clauses in a sentence has, redraft it.

- Try moving the first clause to the end.
  The whole roof gave way and a cascade of giant landsnails, each the size of a small apple, descended upon us before we could do anything intelligent.

- Try moving the final clauses to the beginning.
  A cascade of giant landsnails, each the size of a small apple, descended upon us before we could do anything intelligent when the whole roof gave way.

Compare your versions with the one the writer chose and decide why the writer's sentence creates more suspense.

4 Read the last paragraph again. Explain how the writer's choice of words shows that Gerald Durrell has a positive attitude towards these animals. *(2 marks)*

5 How does the writer's description make the most of this comic situation?
You should write about:
- how the writer builds up suspense
- what happens at the end of the passage
- what comments the narrator makes
- how the noises and movements of the snails are described. *(5 marks)*

91

PRACTICE
C9 Night flight

In this unit you will practise investigating how a writer who is an expert makes specialist information interesting and accessible to a general audience.

KEY POINTS

Investigating how a text has been made entertaining

1. a Read the text on page 94 and study the picture. Then close your books and brainstorm all the information you can remember about shearwaters.
   b Check how much you remembered by looking back at the text. Then talk about what made those pieces of information easy to remember.

In the test you may be asked to read an information text that is written in an entertaining way – an 'infotainment' text. On the one hand, writers know it is important to make sure that the information they write about is easy for readers with little knowledge of the topic to understand. On the other hand, just reading facts can be boring so it is important for the writer to make the information interesting and entertaining to keep readers hooked.

2. Study the example, which is taken from the text, and the annotations on the opposite page to find out how a writer can make information more entertaining for readers.

3. Work in a group. Use the six questions from the annotations opposite to investigate the way the writer made the information in the rest of the first paragraph on page 94 entertaining for readers. Note your answers in a chart like the one below.

Question	Lines in the text	How did the writer make it entertaining?
1 Does the writer link the new information to information that readers will already know?		
2		

4. a Work on your own. Use the same six questions to help you to investigate the writer's techniques in the final paragraph. Make a list of your findings.
   b Compare your findings with a partner and talk about which methods David Attenborough used most successfully in the text.

Check! Work in pairs. What techniques would you advise an expert to use to write an 'infotainment' text explaining how a new invention works?

> Night flight

1 Does the writer link the new information to information that readers will already know?
All readers will know about tripping or stumbling on uneven ground, so it's easy to understand what the nest holes are like.

6 Does the writer use a friendly, chatty style?
Here he talks to readers as if he were a friend giving advice to someone who will visit the island where the shearwaters nest.

5 How has the writer tried to make the text amusing?
The verbs 'flounder' and 'crash', which describe the bird's reaction, make an amusing picture of the clumsy bird trying to hurry away.

They nest in holes in the soft ground and if you are not careful, as you pick your way down through the steeply sloping wood, you either step in one of their holes and trip, or you stumble over a newly emerged bird, in which case it will flounder off in alarm and crash through the blackness into the undergrowth. Like all shearwaters, their legs are placed far back on their bodies. That is the most effective position for propelling them through water. It does, however, mean that they cannot stand upright. The only way they can get about on land is to shuffle forward in an ungainly fashion with their breasts close to the ground.

2 Is any new information linked to the writer's own experiences?
The writer describes stumbling over a bird and frightening it off.

4 Does the writer make it easy for readers to picture information?
The writer appeals to the senses by using the words 'crash' and 'blackness'.

3 How much technical detail and vocabulary does the writer use?
Only a little. Here he explains why the shearwater's legs are placed far back and uses one technical word 'propelling', but the rest is in simpler language.

> C9: Practice

Below is an extract from David Attenborough's book *Life of Birds* that describes how shearwaters struggle to find the right take-off point.

Night flight

In the night, on a small offshore island in Japan, birds wait in line to clamber up a tree trunk. They are streaked shearwaters, sea-birds the size of pigeons. They nest in holes in the soft ground and if you are not careful, as you pick your way down through the steeply sloping wood, you either step in one of their holes and trip, or you stumble over a newly
5 emerged bird, in which case it will flounder off in alarm and crash through the blackness into the undergrowth. Like all shearwaters, their legs are placed far back on their bodies. That is the most effective position for propelling them through water. It does, however, mean that they cannot stand upright. The only way they can get about on land is to shuffle forward in an ungainly fashion with their breasts close to the ground. They make their way
10 down the slope towards a chestnut tree that is particularly suited to their purpose. There they wait their turn to scramble up on to its sloping trunk which is as thick as a telegraph pole. Nose to tail, they inch up it, pushing with their legs, scrabbling with the elbows of their closed wings. The tree has clearly been used in this way for a long time, for its bark is heavily scratched, down to its red underbark.

15 The trunk is hollow. Unluckily for the shearwaters, about ten feet up there is a hole in it. Occasionally, one of the climbers blunders into the hole and drops down the interior. Undeterred by this mishap, it emerges at the bottom and rejoins the queue to start all over again. But most of them manage to avoid this set-back and continue to inch higher and higher up the trunk until some twenty feet above the ground, it bends down towards the
20 horizontal. Having reached that point the birds stop and look about them. They are above the canopy of the surrounding trees and can see out through a gap in the branches towards the moonlit sea. One by one, they open their long narrow wings, lean forward into space and launch themselves into the air. Instantly they are transformed from clumsy halting climbers into superbly competent aeronauts and away they sail into the black
25 night, off to the sea to fish.

> From *Life of Birds* by David Attenborough

> Night flight

> **? HELP | Types of questions**
>
> Before you answer the questions below, read them through and work out which requires you to:
> - select information from the text
> - 'read between the lines'
> - explain why the writer has structured and organised the text in a particular way
> - investigate the writer's language choices
> - explain the overall effect – how the writer's choices affect a reader's response.

Questions

1 Copy the chart below and use information from the text to complete it.

Shearwaters	Facts
Where they live	
How they move	
What they eat	
Where they nest	
What shearwaters are good at	
What shearwaters cannot do	

(3 marks)

2 This text is intended for a general audience. Explain why the comparisons below are well suited to a general audience.

> sea-birds the size of pigeons (line 2)

> [the chestnut tree's] sloping trunk which is as thick as a telegraph pole (lines 11–12)

(2 marks)

3 Explain the effect of presenting these three sentences in this order.

> Like all shearwaters, their legs are placed far back on their bodies.
> That is the most effective position for propelling them through water.
> It does, however, mean that they cannot stand upright. (lines 6–8)

(2 marks)

> C9: Practice

> **HELP | Explaining the order of sentences**
>
> If a question asks you to explain the order of sentences in a text, compare the information you are given first with what you are told last and ask yourself the following questions.
> - What is the effect of placing the information in this order?
> - What contrasts are there between the sort of language the writer has used to begin and end the quotation? Notice things like tone (formal and informal) and vocabulary (technical and everyday words).

4   Explain how the sounds of the words in the last sentence of the text add to the description. *(2 marks)*

> **HELP | The sound of words**
>
> When a question asks you about the sounds of words:
> - think about what information the words give
> - ask yourself if the sounds of the words reinforce the information, e.g. heavy sounds to describe heavy movements, lighter sounds to suggest speed
> - look for examples of onomatopoeia, alliteration and contrast and explain the effect that the words have.

5   How has the writer made this information about shearwaters accessible and interesting for non-expert readers?
    You should write about:
    - the way the text begins and ends
    - the sort of information readers are given
    - the way the birds' behaviour is described
    - how the writer has tried to made the account amusing. *(5 marks)*

↘ Comparing texts

Read the extract 'Things that go scrunch in the night' by Gerald Durrell on page 89 and the extract 'Night flight' by David Attenborough on page 94 again carefully. Both these entertaining non-fiction texts are written by expert naturalists. Compare the ways in which the two writers go about entertaining their audiences. *(3 marks)*

> **HELP**
>
> If a question in the test asks you to compare texts, think about what the main focus of the text is and what impression readers will take with them afterwards. For example, Gerald Durrell's readers are likely to remember Gerald Durrell rather than what the snails are like, whereas David Attenborough's readers will have a stronger impression of what shearwaters are like rather than what he is like.

PRACTICE
C10 The present

In this unit you will practise investigating the way a character can be revealed in a fiction text.

KEY POINTS

Investigating the techniques used to reveal a character

1. Read the text on page 99 and then talk about how you go about investigating what a character is like.

   In the test you may be asked to comment on the way a writer portrays a character. **Start** by searching for details about a character's:
   - appearance
   - dialogue
   - thoughts
   - feelings/attitudes
   - behaviour
   - relationships
   - response to other characters, objects or events.

   Then decide what each detail suggests about the character.

   Of course, writers don't always include all these different types of details. Instead, a writer may prefer to describe a character by focusing on just a few types of details – perhaps mainly describing a character's behaviour rather than his or her appearance.

   Noticing which type of details a writer uses to portray a character helps you to pin down what that writer's technique is.

   Study the example on page 98, which shows how you can work out the way this writer reveals what a character is like.

2. Use the same three steps to work out which techniques the writer uses in the first paragraph of the text on page 99 to reveal what Sam is like.

3. In the text on page 99, which techniques does the writer use to show what Joe is like?

Check! Work in pairs. After you have closed your books, make a flow diagram showing how to investigate the way a character is revealed.

97

> C10: Practice

Step 1 Search for details about the character's:
- appearance
- dialogue
- thoughts
- feelings/attitudes
- behaviour
- relationships
- responses to other characters, objects or events

feelings/attitudes ———

> Sam stood back to admire them. Nothing in the room compared. Even the thickly berried holly, which Ellen had refused to take down on Twelfth Night with the other decorations, was eclipsed. The berries might be 'red as any blood' but the boxing gloves were redder and bloodier and spoke for a power beyond the holly, as Sam knew. He stoked the fire and settled the kettle on it, took the News Chronicle and lit a dog end. But he could not keep his eyes off the snuggling of the large glistening gloves, almost alive as the faintly hissing light played over them; reminded him of new pups.

thoughts ———

behaviour ———

Step 2 When you find a detail, work out what it suggests and notice how it was created.
'The berries might be "red as any blood" but the boxing gloves were redder and bloodier and spoke for a power beyond the holly, as Sam knew.'
This suggests that Sam's faith is in the power the gloves represent – man's physical strength. The writer creates this impression by contrasting two objects – holly berries and boxing gloves – and what they represent.

Step 3 Decide which sort of details the writer has used most.
In this description the writer uses details that show the character's feelings and attitudes, thoughts, behaviour, and response to other characters and objects. The writer doesn't show Sam's appearance or have him speaking. Mainly the description focuses on Sam's feelings and attitudes towards the gloves and the holly and what these represent to him.

> **The present**

This extract is from the opening of Melvyn Bragg's novel *Sons of War*, which is set at the beginning of the twentieth century.

'You can hit as hard as you like and it won't hurt.' Sam whispered the rehearsal as he laid out the big boxing gloves like a bouquet on the table. The words would be addressed to
5   his son but they were aimed at his wife.

The training gloves, blood red, almost new, glistening in the weak white gas-light of late winter afternoon, were nuzzled close, the four knuckle to puffy knuckle, as if waiting for the bell.

10 Sam stood back to admire them. Nothing in the room compared. Even the thickly berried holly, which Ellen had refused to take down on Twelfth Night with the other decorations, was eclipsed. The berries might be **'red as any blood'** but the boxing
15 gloves were redder and bloodier and spoke for a power beyond the holly, as Sam knew. He stoked the fire and settled the kettle on it, took the News Chronicle and lit a **dog end**. But he could not keep his eyes off the snuggling of the large glistening
20 gloves, almost alive as the faintly hissing light played over them; reminded him of new pups. He hummed as he waited – 'Give me five minutes more'. He wanted to extend the time for himself alone with this magnificent present. 'Only five minutes more in your arms'. Blackie air-lifted into his lap so lightly it was almost an embrace, and when Sam stroked her under the chin she purred to match the quiet murmur
25 of the kettle. Sounds full of peace: he felt his mind untense in this quietness that screened no threats.

Joe crashed in first, his face rose-glazed from the raw weather. To Sam's delight he noticed the gloves instantly, a glance of disbelief at his father, and sprang on them. By the time Ellen had taken off her scarf, put down the shopping basket, slipped off her coat and focused, the cavernous gloves were on Joe's seven-year-old paws. He stood there, not much higher than the table, the gloves like gaudy footballs fantastically
30 stuck on the cuffs of his navy blue mac.

'How are you going to get your coat off?'

Joe grinned at his mother and shook his hands. Despite the laces tightly pulled, the gloves dropped to the floor. He unbuttoned, unbelted, flung off his coat in seconds and went down on his knees to cram his hands once more into the hugely padded marvels, which he could not believe were to be his.

35 'You can hit as hard as you like but it won't hurt – not with those.'

'Ding ding. Seconds out!' said Joe, as he took swipes at an imaginary opponent, taking care to clutch hard to the glove on the inside so that it did not fly off.

'I thought boxers were meant to hurt each other,' Ellen replied.

'Special training gloves. Look at the size of them! From Belgium.'

40 Sam seemed transfixed by Joe's childish flailing. He wanted to kneel down and coach him but first there was Ellen.

'It'll help him learn to look after himself without causing damage.'

'You're the one who wants those gloves, Samuel Richardson.'

He looked at her directly and her laughter set off his own.

> From *Sons of War* by Melvyn Bragg

Word bank

'red as any blood' – the holly's redness represents the power of Christian faith. 'Red as any blood' is a line from a Christmas carol that refers to the idea that Jesus Christ's death on the cross supernaturally overcame evil

dog end – a partly smoked cigarette

99

> C10: Practice

❓ HELP | Types of questions

Before you answer the questions below, read them through and work out which requires you to:
- select information from the text
- 'read between the lines'
- look at why the writer has structured and organised the text in a particular way
- investigate the writer's language choices
- look at the overall effect – how the writer's choices affect a reader's response.

↘ Questions

1. Find evidence in the text to prove that:
   a it is not long after Christmas
   b this story takes place a long time ago
   c Joe is seven years old
   d the gloves come from abroad. *(2 marks)*

2. Read lines 1–5 carefully. What do they suggest about Sam and Ellen's relationship? *(2 marks)*

❓ HELP

In question 2 you need to think about the following.
- Who are the boxing gloves for?
- What does the final sentence suggest – what does Ellen feel about Joe boxing? Does Sam know how his wife feels? Does he mind?
- What different things will Sam's words mean to his son and to his wife?

3. Read the first four sentences of the third paragraph again. How has the writer used the boxing gloves and holly to suggest that there are problems in Sam and Ellen's marriage? *(2 marks)*

❓ HELP

When you are working out your answer to a question like question 3, ask yourself relevant questions about the text, such as:
- Which character likes holly?
- What are readers told holly represents?
- Which character likes boxing gloves?
- What is said about the gloves' strength?

4 Below is a complex sentence from the fourth paragraph in the text. Explain the way the order of the clauses is used to reveal the difference between Ellen's character and Joe's character.

> By the time Ellen had taken off her scarf, put down the shopping basket, slipped off her coat and focused, the cavernous gloves were on Joe's seven-year-old paws. (lines 27–29)

(2 marks)

REMEMBER

When you are answering a question like question 4:
- look at what information is given first
- look at what information is given last
- ask yourself: What is emphasised by making readers wait for that information?

5 How has the writer contrasted Ellen's and Sam's characters?

You should write about:
- the different way each of them treats Joe
- Sam's thoughts and feelings towards Ellen
- how Sam and Ellen feel about the gloves and the holly
- the writer's use of language.

(5 marks)

HELP | Linking points

When you are asked to contrast two people or things, link your points together using phrases like these:

however	*in contrast*
but	*on the one hand ... on the other hand ...*

PRACTICE
C11 Box below the line

In this unit you will practise investigating the way an argument is presented.

KEY POINTS

Investigating how an argument is developed

1. a Work on your own. Spend two minutes brainstorming as many different reasons for abolishing homework as you can.
   b Share and discuss the ideas you came up with. Which of them are:
      - opinions?
      - illustrations?
      - speculations?
      - facts?
      - examples?
   c Read the text on page 104. What is this argument about?

In the test when you read a text that develops an argument (like the one you've just read), you need to follow these steps.

Step 1 Search the text for the way that different points are:

- **organised**

  How does the writer:
  a introduce the argument (usually in the first paragraph)?
  b carry the argument forward (in each paragraph)?
  c conclude the argument (usually in the final paragraph)?

- **supported**

  What examples, facts, reasons, illustrations or evidence has the writer given to support each point?

- **linked**

  Find the connectives and link words. Are paragraphs linked or only points within paragraphs? Does this make the argument flow well?

- **expressed**

  What sort of vocabulary and sentences has the writer used? For example, look for emotive language, formal or informal language, rhetorical questions.

- **presented**

  What features are used to organise the text and to emphasise points? For example, look for headings, italics, bold, underlining, etc.

Step 2 When you notice something, work out what impression it creates.

2. Study the example opposite, which is taken from a text about boxing, and find out how to use these steps to investigate the way an argument is developed.
3. Using the questions on the opposite page to help you, make notes on how the argument is developed in the 3rd and 4th paragraphs of the text on page 104.
4. Read the 5th, 6th, 7th and 8th paragraphs of the text on page 104. What is different about the way the argument is developed here? Why is this?

Check! Close your books. List the five features you need to notice when you are asked about how an argument is developed.

> Box below the line

1 How is the argument organised?
The argument is summed up in the first paragraph. Then the writer goes on to give his reason for this in the following paragraph. This makes the argument seem logical and well thought through.

3 How are links made between points?
In the first paragraph, the writer uses 'just as ... so ...' to compare the ideas. This makes it seem a balanced and reasonable point of view.
No link words are used to begin the second paragraph, which explains why the new rule is needed. Perhaps the writer thinks the link is so obvious that it doesn't need reinforcing?

In boxing, just as the belt is the line *below* which a blow may not be landed, so the collar should be the line *above* which a blow may not be landed.

'Evidence that blows to the head can trigger future Alzheimer's Disease'

There is growing disquiet about the head injuries sustained by professional and amateur boxers, and recent evidence that blows to the head can trigger future Alzheimer's Disease.

2 How are points supported?
The first part of the argument is supported first by reason, then by the facts and evidence given in the second paragraph. This makes the argument seem well supported.

4 What sort of language is used?
The language is formal and serious. The phrase 'growing disquiet' is calm rather than emotive or sensational. This helps to make the reader take the argument seriously.

5 How are presentational features used?
The writer has put the prepositions 'above' and 'below' in italics, which helps to emphasise the point.
A quotation from the second paragraph is emphasised by being printed in bold as a sub-heading above the second paragraph. This brings it to the reader's attention quickly and emphasises what is at stake, because Alzheimer's is such a terrible disease.

> C11: Practice

This article is written by the Reverand John Worthington. He is putting forward arguments in favour of changing the rules of boxing.

Boxing – blows below the collar only

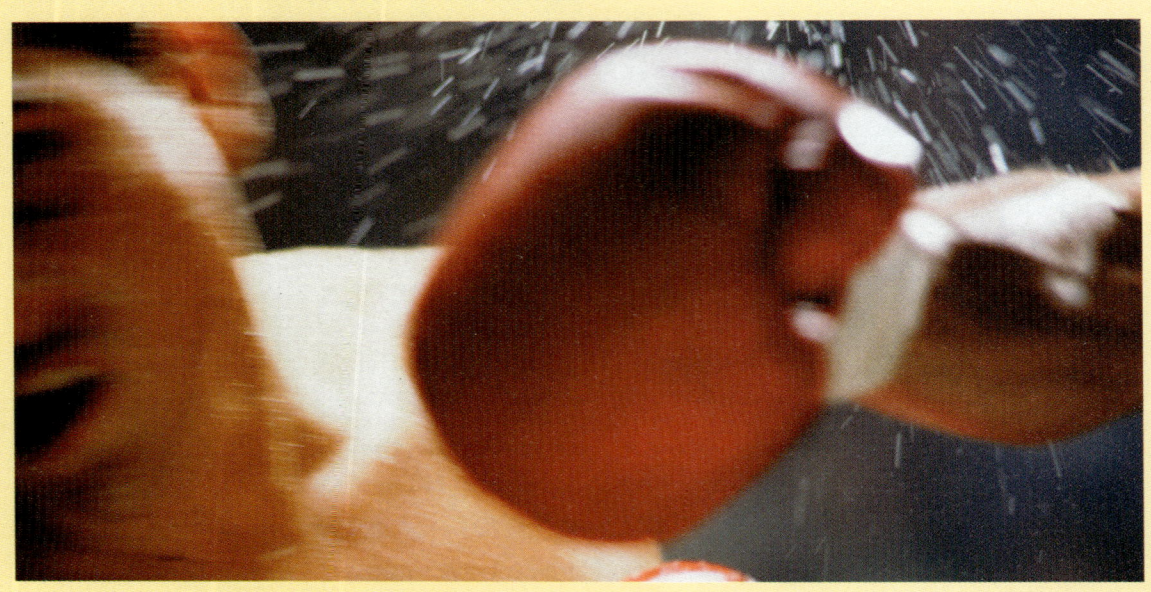

In boxing, just as the belt is the line *below* which a blow may not be landed, so the collar should be the line *above* which a blow may not be landed.

'Evidence that blows to the head can trigger future Alzheimer's Disease'

There is growing disquiet about the head injuries sustained by professional and amateur boxers, and recent evidence that blows to the head can trigger future Alzheimer's Disease.

Among changes to the rules of boxing in the past 150 or so years have been: (1) The introduction of rounds, instead of a continuous fight until one man could fight no more or was knocked out. (2) The banning of bare knuckle fights with the introduction of muffled hands, and then boxing gloves. (Fists as well as heads could be damaged for life.) (3) The banning of head butting. (4) The introduction of not hitting below the belt.

None of the above were easily accepted by **the fancy** at the time.

The main vested interests affected by this new proposal are boxers, boxing promoters, bookmakers, manufacturers and ancillary workers. They should all realise that boxing is on shaky ground. The anti-boxing lobby is alive and may get stronger, but if those interested in the continuance of boxing will take on board this 'limited target' idea, their financial stake in boxing will be safe.

Boxers will never again have the dread of a 'bad' brain scan or permanent eye damage hanging over them.

Boxing will continue to meet the needs of the aggressive spirit of the public and of young men. Amateur boxing would be happy to fall into line and might well increase in popularity in the services and schools.

If a spirited lead is given by the United Kingdom with this idea, it will no doubt be followed worldwide.

Rev. John Worthington

Word bank
the fancy – fans of boxing

> From 'Boxing – blows beneath the collar only' by the Reverand John Worthington

> Box below the line

❓ HELP | Types of questions

Before you answer the questions below, read them through and work out which requires you to:

- select information from the text
- 'read between the lines'
- look at why the writer has structured and organised the text in a particular way
- investigate the writer's language choices
- look at the overall effect – how the writer's choices affect a reader's response.

↘ Questions

1. In what order are the following points argued in the text?
   a. If the UK adopts this approach to boxing, so will the rest of the world.
   b. There is already a line below which you can't hit.
   c. Blows to the head can cause Alzheimer's Disease.
   d. The new rule would help to keep boxers safe from harm.
   e. The new rule would make boxing more popular.
   f. It makes good business sense to change the rules. *(2 marks)*

2. What does the writer suggest about the change in the rules that he would like to see when he points out that: 'None of the above were easily accepted by the fancy at the time'? (lines 21–22) *(1 mark)*

3. a. Why is the text printed in bold between the first and second paragraphs? *(1 mark)*

   b. Many of the paragraphs are single sentences. What is the effect of setting out the argument like this? *(2 marks)*

4. Why does the writer change to a different verb tense in:
   - the third paragraph? (lines 23–31)
   - the final three paragraphs? (lines 32–42) *(2 marks)*

❓ HELP | Changes in verb tense

When you are asked about the reason for changes in verb tense, work out your ideas by:

- noticing whether the text before the part you are asked about is in the past, present or future tense
- recognising how the tense has changed in the part you are asked about
- deciding what job is done by the part of the text you are asked about.

> C11: Practice

5 How does the writer develop his argument about introducing a new rule into boxing?
You should write about:
- how the text is organised
- the different ways the writer supports his points
- the way the writer links his points
- the writer's use of language.

(5 marks)

HELP | Choice of language

When you are asked to write about the way language is used in an argument text, think about:

- what kind of vocabulary the writer has used, for example: emotive, sensational, formal, academic, etc.
- what kind of attitude is created by the writer's choice of words, for example: reasonable, emotional, calm, aggressive, etc.

PRACTICE
C12 Spit or swallow?

In this unit you will practise investigating the way writers encourage readers to trust them.

KEY POINTS

Investigating the way writers encourage readers to trust them

1   a   Look at the cartoon below. Whose advice should the boy listen to? Why?

[Cartoon: A boy asks "Should I be a boxer?" Four people respond: a blonde woman says "No, you'll just get your face smashed up!"; a man in a white coat says "Boxing can seriously damage your health."; a boxer with red gloves says "It's great if you win, but if you don't there's no money."; a man in a striped shirt says "You've got good potential if you train properly."]

   b   Read the text on page 109. Should boxers always spit or swallow? Give reasons for your answer.

In the test you may be asked to comment on the way the writer of an article, such as the one you just read, creates an impression of what he or she is like and whether what they say can be trusted. Writers who want readers to trust them may:

- **prove they are an expert** so that readers will trust the information they give. They may refer to their qualifications, talk about their professional experience, use technical terms, etc.
- **use calm, rational language** rather than sensational or emotive language so that readers won't feel they are being provoked
- make sure that their **points are well organised and supported**
- **encourage readers to agree** with them, talking about common experiences so readers think 'Yes, I've noticed that too'
- **have a respectful and positive attitude** towards the subject and reader.

107

> C12: Practice

2 Read the example below and find out how to spot which techniques a writer is using to encourage readers to trust what is said in the text.

3 Read the underlined details in the example. Make a chart showing how each detail adds to the impression that this writer can be trusted.

4 Work in groups. Each group should study one of the other paragraphs of the text on page 109 to discover how details create the impression that the advice can be trusted. Afterwards each group should share its findings with the class.

Check! What advice would you give to a writer who wants readers to trust his or her advice?

Step 1 Search the text for relevant details.
Step 2 Ask yourself: In what way will this detail encourage readers to trust the writer?

1 This heading points out what the issue is, but because it's put in a jokey way and written by a doctor it reassures readers that he won't be writing things they can't understand.

2 Calling himself by his nickname makes the writer sound approachable. Including his qualification reassures readers that he is an expert.

3 Starting off with this phrase tells readers that he is well known for giving advice, so he can be trusted.

4 This suggests that the writer really knows about boxing in depth.

The ultimate question: spit or swallow?

By Flip Homansky MD

I am frequently asked what is the best replacement fluid during fights. The answer is that the type of fluid is less important than actually getting your fighter to come in well hydrated and to drink enough of anything to prevent dehydration. Boxing has historically treated water as simply something to rinse the mouthpiece with. The water bottle seems to be used mainly to drench the fighter. I don't care how much is poured over a kid's head – he can't absorb it through his skin.

I watch in wonderment as a small lake forms in each corner. I do believe that I have actually seen wooden stools warp from the inundation. After this proper drenching, the boxer very carefully washes his mouth out and daintily spits in the general vicinity of the spit bucket.

108

The text below is taken from a website where a doctor gives advice to boxers.

The ultimate question: spit or swallow?

By Flip Homansky MD

I am frequently asked what is the best replacement fluid during fights. The answer is that the type of fluid is less important than actually getting your fighter to come in well hydrated and to drink enough of anything to prevent dehydration. Boxing has historically treated water as simply something to rinse the mouthpiece with. The water bottle seems to be used mainly to drench the fighter. I don't care how much is poured over a kid's head – he can't absorb it through his skin.

I watch in wonderment as a small lake forms in each corner. I do believe that I have actually seen wooden stools warp from the inundation. After this proper drenching, the boxer very carefully washes his mouth out and daintily spits in the general vicinity of the spit bucket.

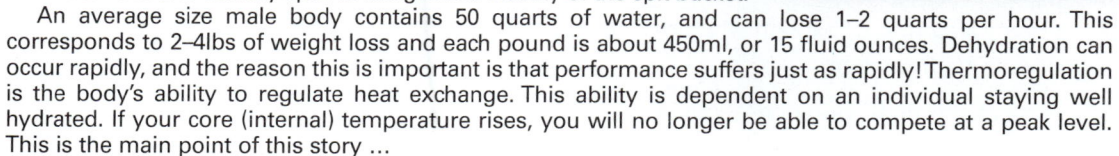

An average size male body contains 50 quarts of water, and can lose 1–2 quarts per hour. This corresponds to 2–4lbs of weight loss and each pound is about 450ml, or 15 fluid ounces. Dehydration can occur rapidly, and the reason this is important is that performance suffers just as rapidly! Thermoregulation is the body's ability to regulate heat exchange. This ability is dependent on an individual staying well hydrated. If your core (internal) temperature rises, you will no longer be able to compete at a peak level. This is the main point of this story …

- each quart of fluid lost = your heart rate increases by 8 beats
- cardiac output declines by 1 liter/min
- core temperature rises by 0.3 degrees
- osmolality increases
- 1% dehydrated – performance begins suffering
- 4% dehydrated – performance cut by 20 to 30%
- 5 to 6% – loss of further thermoregulation, weakness and fatigue
- 7% – collapse

The key is to stay hydrated and never get behind the curve. Go into the bout in as perfect fluid and electrolyte balance as possible. If you have lost a great deal of weight and 'dried out' for the weigh-in, then this is almost impossible. Remember that! You should consume at least 17 ounces of water before any strenuous exercise. Drink especially between each round, and after the fight. I believe drinking anything is more important than what you drink. Water is fine.

I have no problem if you want to drink electrolyte solutions like Gatorade or Pedialyte, but I don't feel they are necessary in boxing. These commercial products contain predominantly water combined with electrolytes and carbohydrates. Carbohydrates are known to slow the rate of gastric emptying. This will decrease the rate of absorption of water from the gut. Carbohydrate ingestion clearly improves performance in events lasting longer than 90 minutes (Coggan and Coyle; Exercise, Sports Science Review – volume 19, 1991). Our longest matches are only 36 minutes of actual activity.

What our boxers need is to come into the contest well hydrated and to replace the fluids they lose during the match. I don't believe electrolytes during that short period are relevant, but shouldn't hurt. **Carbs** may indeed slow down our ability to use the water we drink. If the fighter is to use Gatorade, then I would dilute it with water. The temperature should be slightly cool, not warm or icy.

A fighter must train his body to accept this regimen. Never force someone to drink during a contest if he hasn't been doing this in training, and especially during sparring. Periods of intensive training that last over an hour will benefit from electrolyte replacement.

I hope the above has convinced you that it is almost always better to swallow …

> From 'The ultimate question: spit or swallow' by Flip Homansky MD

Word bank

MD – medical doctor

osmolality increases – blood fluids become more concentrated, which makes it harder for the body's cells to absorb what they need

carbs – short for 'carbohydrates'

> C12: Practice

> **? HELP | Types of questions**
>
> Before you answer the questions below, read them through and work out which requires you to:
> - select information from the text
> - 'read between the lines'
> - look at why the writer has structured and organised the text in a particular way
> - investigate the writer's language choices
> - look at the overall effect – how the writer's choices affect a reader's response.

↘ Questions

1. List two reasons why dehydration is a problem for boxers. *(1 mark)*

2. From paragraph 6, explain why drinking electrolyte solutions is unlikely to improve a boxer's performance. *(2 marks)*

3. Look at the final sentence. Explain why this is an effective way to end the text. *(2 marks)*

> **? HELP | Explaining text endings**
>
> When you are asked about the way a text ends, you should first look back at the way it started. Is there an obvious link? Then think about the purpose of the ending, for example does it sum up the writer's point of view or leave readers with a fresh point to think about?

4. From the first three paragraphs, pick out and explain three phrases that help to create the impression that this advice is written by an expert. *(3 marks)*

> **? HELP**
>
> When you have found the three phrases and are ready explain them, you could use the following sentence starters to help you express your answer clearly.
> *The writer creates the impression that …*
> *He does this by using the words … This suggests that …*

5 How does the writer try to make sure that readers will trust his advice?
You should write about:
- what the writer reveals about himself
- how the writer supports his point of view
- the variety of vocabulary the writer uses
- the way the text is organised.

(5 marks)

REMEMBER

When you are answering a question like question 5:
- pick out the key words in the question
- make sure that your answer is thorough by turning each prompt into a question to ask yourself, e.g. what does the writer reveal about himself that will help readers to trust his advice?
- when you make a point, give evidence from the text and explain how that evidence supports your point
- try to write your answer as a mini argument: introduce what your answer is about, link your points (supported by evidence) together and end with a concluding sentence.

Comparing texts

Read 'Boxing – blows below the collar only' on page 104 and 'The ultimate question: spit or swallow' on page 109 carefully. Both texts give reasons for the changes they suggest. Explain **one** similarity and **two** differences in the way the writers support their points of view.

(3 marks)

HELP

Work out what different types of evidence are used to support the writer's point of view in each text, for example:
- medical evidence
- past experience
- experts' views
- statistics
- illustrations.

PRACTICE
C13 Home They Brought Her Warrior

In this unit you will practise making sense of an unfamiliar setting by investigating the theme in a pre-1914 poem.

KEY POINTS

Investigating the theme in a pre-1914 text

1. a What do you do when you read a pre-1914 text on your own?
   b Read the text on page 114 and use the following steps to help you work out what the poem is about. These same four steps can be used to help you understand other difficult texts.

Step 1 Get an overview of what, when and where the text is about.
Read the text through quickly once and try to work out:
- What is it about?

It sounds as if it's about a funeral.
- When is it set?

A very long time ago – when there were warriors and maidens. The introduction said mediaeval times.
- Where is it set?

At the warrior's home. The widow has lots of maidens so they must be well off.

Step 2 Try to remember what you already know about the time, place or situation that the text is about.
In mediaeval times there were knights – is it the same sort of time as Robin Hood or King Arthur? Women wore long dresses. Battles were fought with swords.

Step 3 Search for what you *can* understand.
Read the text sentence by sentence. Keep asking: What does this tell me?

Step 4 Use what you *do* know to help you to work out what you *don't* know.
Read the text again slowly, trying to work out the meaning of any difficult words or sentences. As you read, use what you already know and what you have understood to help you to work out the things you are not sure about.

Don't worry if you can't understand everything!

In the test you may be asked to respond to the theme in a pre-1914 text that you have not seen before. As you start reading, bear in mind the following points.

> Home They Brought Her Warrior

- Some things change with time, such as the clothes that people wear, what people call each other and which words are fashionable to use. When you read a pre-1914 text, all this can make it seem very unfamiliar.
- However, the ideas at the heart of a pre-1914 text will be familiar to you because the way human beings behave and feel does not really change over time. For centuries people have worried about the same kinds of things – family, friendships, love, death – and have felt the same emotions that we feel today.
- Writers of pre-1914 texts use many of the same techniques you already know about, for example they might use opposites to tell readers what young people think is important versus what old people think is important.
- Writers of pre-1914 poems use the same poetic devices – imagery, rhythm, rhyme, and so on – as poets do today. They just build their poems with words or details that are less familiar to you.

2 Read the example below and find out how you can work out the theme of a poem and how the writer has used language.

Step 1 As you read, change the order of the words to help you to work out what a sentence means.
They brought her dead warrior home.

Home They Brought Her Warrior

Home they brought her warrior dead:
   She nor swoon'd, nor utter'd cry:
All her maidens, watching, said,
   'She must weep or she will die.'

Step 2 Sum up in your own words what each paragraph or stanza is about.
This woman's husband is dead and the people around her are worried because she is not showing that she is upset. They think it's bad for her.

Step 3 Decide what theme(s) the whole text is about.
This text is about death, the sadness of war and how to grieve.

Step 4 Search for opposites that are used to explore the theme.
Servants who know how a widow should behave versus the lady of the house who isn't doing what they expect.

Step 5 Ask yourself: What do any poetic devices add to the theme?
The rhythm of these lines is slow and the sounds of the words add to the feeling of sadness – these techniques emphasise the theme of grief.

3 Work in a group. Copy the second and third stanzas of the poem on page 114 on to the centre of a page. Make notes around each stanza as you work out:
   a) what it is about b) what opposites are used c) how it is written.

4 Work as a class. Follow the steps above and make notes on what the final stanza is about and the way it is written.

Check! Make a mindmap to help you remember how to investigate the way a theme is studied in an older text.

> C13: Practice

This poem by Alfred, Lord Tennyson was written in the 19th century, but is set in mediaeval times.

Home They Brought Her Warrior

Home they brought her **warrior** dead:
    She nor swoon'd, nor utter'd cry:
All her maidens, watching, said,
    'She must weep or she will die.'

5   Then they praised him, soft and low,
    Call'd him worthy to be loved,
Truest friend and noblest foe;
    Yet she neither spoke nor moved.

Stole a maiden from her place,
10   Lightly to the warrior stept,
Took the **face-cloth** from the face;
    Yet she neither moved nor wept.

Rose a **nurse** of ninety years,
    Set his child upon her knee –
15 Like summer **tempest** came her tears –
    'Sweet my child, I live for thee.'

Alfred, Lord Tennyson

Word bank
warrior – a brave soldier
face-cloth – when a body was prepared for burial, a cloth was placed over the face so that it could not be seen
nurse – a child's nanny
tempest – storm

> Home They Brought Her Warrior

↴ Questions

1. In what order do the following events happen in the poem?
   a. The widow holds her child.
   b. The soldier's body is brought home.
   c. The maidens worry about how the widow is behaving.
   d. The soldier's face is uncovered.
   e. The maidens tell the widow what a great man the soldier was. *(2 marks)*

2. The widow does not cry until the end of the last stanza. What does this suggest about her feelings about her husband's death? *(2 marks)*

3. What does the writer emphasise by his choice of word order in the first line? *(2 marks)*

❓ HELP

When thinking about word order in a poem, remember that readers usually notice the first and last words in a line.

4. What does the image in line 15 suggest about the widow's grief? *(2 marks)*

5. How has the writer made readers think about the effects of war in this poem?
   You should write about:
   - how the different characters react to the death of the soldier
   - what the maidens do to try to make the widow cry
   - what does and doesn't make the widow grieve
   - the way the poem is written. *(5 marks)*

❓ HELP | Writing about the way a poem is written

When you are thinking about the way a poem is written, look for poetic devices and explain how they are relevant to the question. When you spot a poetic device, keep asking yourself questions about how it is used.

For example, this poem is written in stanzas.
- How do stanzas help to separate the events in the narrative?
- How do stanzas help to emphasise the different points made about the impact of war on families?
- What is the impact of presenting the stanzas in this particular order?

115

PRACTICE
C14 Defeat

In this unit you will practise investigating bias in a recount text.

KEY POINTS

Investigating a biased text

1. a What is bias?
    b Can you give any examples of texts that are biased, e.g. political pamphlets?
    c Read the text on pages 118–119. Do you think it is biased? Give reasons for your answer.

A writer may have several purposes when writing a text – to entertain as well as inform, to analyse as well as describe. A writer may also want to present a biased point of view. Sometimes bias is obvious and easy to spot, such as in advertisements that are biased in favour of the product they are selling, because they tell you only positive things about it.

Other biased texts are more subtle and it may not be so obvious that a biased viewpoint is being presented. When we read a text and are unaware that it is biased, we may believe that it is balanced and reliable. We may accept its information and ideas without questioning them.

To understand whether a text is biased or not you need to work out the writer's standpoint – who is the writer and what does he or she believe? Then you need to search the text to see whether a balanced view is presented or whether the text gives only information that agrees with the writer's point of view.

2. Read the example opposite, and check that you know how to investigate bias in a text.

3. Work in a group. Read paragraphs 2 and 3 from the text on page 118 and work out whether the text is biased. Make notes about how any bias is created. Use the steps opposite to help you.

4. Work in pairs. Examine paragraph 4 from the text on page 119 and explain how the writer uses language to show he is critical of the Japanese army by looking at:
    - the way questions are used
    - the facts readers are told
    - the writer's opinions.

5. Work as a class. If the writer were not biased, what other sorts of information might he have included in his account of the Japanese defeat at Kohima Ridge?

Check!
- How can you work out whether a text is biased?
- Which features help you understand how bias is created?

Step 1 Identify the bias.
- What is the writer's standpoint?
  He is a Japanese soldier whose regiment was defeated by the British at Kohima Ridge.
- What is the writer's purpose?
  To defend his regiment's failure to prevent Kohima Ridge from being captured.
- Are different point(s) of view presented?
  No, only the Japanese soldier's point of view. A British soldier might give different reasons for his army's success. Someone who was neither British nor Japanese might give a different view again.

Step 2 Examine how the bias is created. Ask these questions:

Defeat

It was not surprising that in the middle of May the British 2nd Division found it possible to recapture the hills of the Kohima Ridge from us. Our losses had been dreadful. Our soldiers fought bravely, but they had no rations, no rifle or machine-gun ammunition, no artillery shells for the guns to fire. And, above all, they had no support from rear echelons. How could they have continued in such dreadful circumstances? The monsoon season had started and the Kohima region is notorious for having the heaviest rainfall in the world. In the unceasing rain there was no shelter. If one hid beneath a tree the enemy's shells would destroy not just that tree but everything around it. There was only one consolation: the rains reduced the firing but it resumed as soon as the rain stopped.

- What evidence is selected?
  Only details about the Japanese problems are given as reasons for the defeat. Nothing is said about what the British did.
- Look at the choice of language.
  This phrase does not give the British army any praise or credit for what happened.
- What opinions are given?
  The soldier admires only his own side.
- What reasons are given?
  Only reasons that were beyond his regiment's control are given, such as the lack of supplies, support, bad weather, etc.
- What conclusions are drawn?
  This conclusion seems reasonable. However, the evidence has been carefully selected to support this point of view. Using a rhetorical question encourages readers to agree.
- Look at the use of evocative description/illustrations.
  The bad conditions are made to sound extreme.

> C14: Practice

In the text below a Japanese soldier describes his experiences in Burma in World War II when his regiment suffered defeat at the hands of the British army.

Defeat

It was not surprising that in the middle of May the British 2nd Division found it possible to recapture the hills of the Kohima Ridge from us. Our losses had been dreadful. Our soldiers fought bravely, but they had no rations, no rifle or machine-gun ammunition, no artillery shells for the guns to fire. And, above all, they had no support from rear **echelons**. How could they have continued in such dreadful circumstances? The monsoon season had started and the Kohima region is notorious for having the heaviest rainfall in the world. In the unceasing rain there was no shelter. If one hid beneath a tree the enemy's shells would destroy not just that tree but everything around it. There was only one consolation: the rains reduced the firing but it resumed as soon as the rain stopped.

It was impossible to cook rice in the rain. Sometimes we made a fire from undergrowth and boiled vegetable matter as the only means we had of staving off our terrible hunger. When the shelling began again we entered our 'octopus traps' – holes dug in the ground to a soldier's height – but the rain flooded in so that we were chest-high in water and had to climb out. We felt we had arrived at the very limit of our endurance.

At the beginning of the Imphal Operation the regiment was 3,800 strong. When our general gave the order to withdraw to the east we were reduced to just a few hundreds still alive. Without shelter from the rains, with boots that had rotted and had to be bound with grass, we began to trudge along the deep mud paths carrying our rifles without ammunition, leaning on sticks to support our weak bodies. Our medical corps men slipped and slid as they carried the sick and wounded on stretchers or supported the 'walking wounded'. Some of the orderlies were themselves so weak that they fell to the ground again and again until their physical and moral endurance was at an end, so that when a sick man cried out in pain they simply said, 'If you complain we'll just let you go, and throw you and the stretcher down the cliff side.'

118

> Defeat

Icy rain fell mercilessly on us and we lived day and night drenched to the skin and pierced with cold. I remember how we longed for a place, any place at all, where we could take shelter and rest. Once we found a tent in the jungle; inside it were the bodies of six nurses. We had never imagined there would be female victims, especially
45 so far over the Arakan Mountains. Why, we asked one another, had the army not taken the nurses to a place of safety? In another tent we found the bodies of three soldiers who had taken their own lives. How could one ever forget such terrible, distressing sights as the dead nurses, and the soldiers who had taken their own lives? All I could do was to swear to myself that, somehow, I would survive.

> Adapted from *Tales by Japanese Soldiers* by Kazuo Tamayama and John Nunneley

Word bank

echelons – groups of soldiers

Questions

1. List two pieces of information from the text about the area of land called Kohima and its weather. *(1 mark)*

2. **a** From the second paragraph, explain why the soldiers couldn't cook rice. *(1 mark)*

   b From the third paragraph, explain why the soldiers' boots were bound with grass. *(1 mark)*

   c From the last paragraph, explain why the writer was so determined to survive. *(1 mark)*

3. The writer uses three questions in the text (one in the first paragraph and two in the fourth paragraph). Explain what effect each question has on readers. *(3 marks)*

HELP | Considering the impact of questions

Think about:

- how readers are likely to answer rhetorical questions – are they encouraged to agree or disagree with the writer?
- how readers might respond to a character's questions – does it make them have greater empathy with the character and think, 'Yes, that's how I'd feel, too'?

> C14: Practice

4   How does the writer's choice of words in the following sentence from the start of paragraph 4 create an evocative description?

> Icy rain fell mercilessly on us and we lived day and night drenched to the skin and pierced with cold.

(3 marks)

> **! REMEMBER**
>
> To score maximum marks on a question about the writer's choice of words, you need to:
> → pinpoint the powerful descriptive words
>   *For example, in the sentence above 'icy' is a powerful word.*
> → decide what impact each word has
>   *'Icy' makes you feel sorry for the soldiers because you can imagine what it's like to have freezing cold water falling on you.*
> → explain why each word has that impact.
>   *Describing icy cold water in this way appeals to the senses, which everyone can understand.*

5   How has the writer created bias in his analysis of the recapture of Kohima Ridge and the defeat of his regiment?
   You should write about:
   • what readers are told about Kohima and events during that time
   • how the problems and hardships faced by the soldiers are explained
   • what the Japanese soldier thinks about the situation
   • the way he organises the text
   • the use of language.

(5 marks)

PRACTICE
C15 Mum's Army

In this unit you will practise investigating the way image is created in a media text through the choice of vocabulary.

KEY POINTS

Investigating the way image is created in a media text

1. a Read the text on page 123. Why do you think the writer made the women sound like soldiers?
   b Think of some people who have been in the news lately. What image do they have in the press?

In the test you may be asked to examine the impression that a media text gives of its subject. For example, in the newspaper article on page 123 the group of women tackling inner-city crime are presented as soldiers in an army. This image is created to make the story more interesting and entertaining for readers.

When you examine how an image is created, you should think about the writer's viewpoint (in this case, that the women are brave and heroic) and the way in which vocabulary and pictures are chosen to create the same impression all the way through the text.

2. Read the example on page 122, which is taken from the article on page 123, and find out how to examine the way in which an impression is created in a media text.

3. Work in groups. Study what Mrs Hellmich says in the text on page 123. How do her words present a different image of the group of women?

4. Look at the last three paragraphs of the article on page 123. How does the writer make sure that readers finish the article still thinking of the women as an army?

5. Talk about how you could go about changing the image of the SAFE group in this article if you wanted to make them seem less powerful. You could use these ideas to help you:
   - choose different vocabulary
   - use different photographs.

Check! What advice would you give to a journalist who wanted to create the impression that someone was:
   a extremely athletic?
   b mysterious?

> C15: Practice

Step 1 Sum up the impression created in the text.
There is a war going on (against crime) and these women are like a conquering army.

Step 2 Examine the writer's choice of vocabulary to help you to work out how the impression is created.
The words highlighted in blue associated with the women are military or to do with the police.
The words highlighted in red describe the criminals emphasise the bad behaviour and the way they terrorise the community.

Step 3 Decide how the impression is reinforced through the pictures.
The women are shown looking tough. They aren't smiling and look serious. The shot is taken so that the reader is looking up at them. The women are outside on patrol in the streets.

Armed with nothing but a mobile phone, this team of women crack down on thugs

How a Mum's Army patrol brought safety to the city where fear stalked the streets

By **Mark Lister**

The band of women have been dubbed 'Mum's Army' – but they are far from being a joke. Together they have helped reduce crime in a troubled inner-city that is torn by racial tension.

As they patrol the streets of Bradford – a city which saw the worst rioting in Britain for decades, last year – the women have quietly gone about restoring law and order.

Drug-pushers were openly dealing on street corners and swaggering youths struck fear into elderly and young residents alike in the days following the violence.

122

The newspaper article below reports on a group of women who are battling against inner-city crime.

Armed with nothing but a mobile phone, this team of women crack down on thugs

How a Mum's Army patrol brought safety to the city where fear stalked the streets

By **Mark Lister**

CRUSADING AGAINST CRIME: Shazlya Younas and Elizabeth Hellmich are familiar figures patrolling the troubled areas of racially torn Bradford

The band of women have been dubbed 'Mum's Army' – but they are far from being a joke. Together they have helped reduce crime in a troubled inner-city that is torn by racial tension.

As they patrol the streets of Bradford – a city which saw the worst rioting in Britain for decades, last year – the women have quietly gone about restoring law and order.

Drug-pushers were openly dealing on street corners and swaggering youths struck fear into elderly and young residents alike in the days following the violence.

But now the 32-strong team of volunteers have become the eyes and ears of West Yorkshire Police in the city's once crime-ravaged areas of Manningham, Girlington and Heaton.

The police have even issued the women with mobile phones – giving them a hot-line to operations control in case they witness a crime taking place.

The crusade was begun by mother-of-two Elizabeth Hellmich, 49, in the aftermath of last summer's riots, which saw hundreds of youths – mostly Asian – destroy the reputation of the city she loved as they ran amok in the streets.

Mrs Hellmich said: 'There were areas, such as the local park, which were thought of as "no go" areas.

'The young men who had rioted and were committing crimes were mother's sons, nephews or young women's husbands.

'In the past, women had sheltered these people from the police, but we decided to co-operate with the police and stand up to the criminals.'

Now Asian and white women, aged from 19 to 75, have united in SAFE (Safe Areas For Everyone) to report immediately to the police any drug dealing, car theft, assaults or vandalism they see.

Mrs Hellmich said: 'We are not vigilantes but together with the police we aim to crack down on crime and bring the area back up.'

The Home Office-backed project has been given an £11,000 grant to train the women in First Aid, self defence and negotiating techniques.

Now Mrs Hellmich is a familiar sight as, together with her English springer spaniel Ella, she pounds her local beat on the look-out for trouble.

She said: 'We don't tackle anybody who could be violent, but we do step in if we see young children up to no good.'

With the backing of police and growing interest in the movement, the army is set to swell to about 150 members. Police believe that middle-aged women are ideal for keeping youngsters under control because they are less confrontational than men.

Chief Superintendent Phil Read, divisional commander for Bradford North police, said: 'Parental involvement is crucial in dealing with such problems and it is good news for the whole of Bradford that Asian women are taking a lead.'

If the pilot project is successful, 'Mum's Armies' could be launched around the country.

> C15: Practice

↘ Questions

1. In which areas of Bradford does this group of women operate? *(1 mark)*
2. Read paragraphs 6 to 10 again. What caused the women to change their behaviour? *(2 marks)*

❓ HELP | Making a deduction

When you need to deduce something, as in question 2 above, ask yourself questions about the text to help you to work out your answer. In this case think carefully about:

- why the women behaved differently in the past
- the consequences of the riots
- the name of the new group.

3. How does the order of phrases used in the strapline help to engage the reader's interest? *(2 marks)*

❗ REMEMBER

A strapline is the line of text that comes above the headline of a newspaper story. It usually gives readers a very concise summary of what the story is about and is written in a way that will grab their interest.

4. What impact does the underlined noun phrase in the sentence below have on readers? How does the writer achieve this impact?

> 'Together they have helped reduce crime in a <u>troubled inner-city that is torn by racial tension</u>.' (paragraph 1)

(2 marks)

❓ HELP | Examining the impact of a noun phrase

First look closely at the words and what they mean. Notice whether any poetic device is used. Think about what is being emphasised. In this case:

- the adjective used is 'troubled'
- the verb used is 'torn' – this is short and violent sounding
- alliteration is created by the repetition of 't' sounds ('troubled', 'torn', 'tension').

Then decide what impact these words have on the reader.

5 How does the writer create the impression that these women are a force to be reckoned with?

You should write about:
- the use of presentational features, such as pictures and headlines
- what readers are told about the women's achievements
- what readers are told about the problems in Bradford
- the writer's vocabulary choices.

(5 marks)

↘ Comparing texts

Read the extract 'Defeat' on pages 118–119 and the article about Mum's Army on page 123 carefully. Both writers show bias in their texts. Explain three ways in which readers can tell that both texts are biased.

(3 marks)

> **REMEMBER | Examining bias**
>
> When you are examining bias in a text, think about:
> - the standpoint the text is written from
> - the evidence that is given
> - whose opinions are presented (and whose are not)
> - the reasons readers are given (and any that might have been left out)
> - conclusions that are drawn
> - how things are described.
>
> For more help with examining bias, look at page 31.

PRACTICE
C16 Face to face

In this unit you will practise responding to the genre features of a text.

KEY POINTS

Responding to the genre features of a text

1.
   a. Make a list of story genres that you have read or watched, for example science fiction, horror stories, etc. Rank them in order, beginning with the genre that you enjoy most. Be ready to give reasons for your choices.
   b. Read the text on pages 128–129. What genre do you think it belongs to?
   c. Talk about how a writer can combine in one story the features from two genres, such as horror and science fiction.

Writers know that readers often choose a book because it belongs to a genre that they enjoy reading. So writers might use typical genre features but try to give them a new slant. For example, a horror story has to have a monster but what will it be like? It could be a vampire, a mummy, a wolf or something more unusual like a car with strange powers. What will the monster want? What problems will it cause? Good writers can find plenty of scope to be original and creative but still be true to the features of a particular genre. Writers might also blend two genres together – such as horror and fantasy or mystery and romance.

Readers quickly recognise the features of genres and this builds up a sense of expectation. They might think, 'Oh good, it's a horror story!' and this makes them want to read on. At the same time readers enjoy what is different about the story they are reading – the way one writer builds suspense or the way another blends features from two genres.

2. Read the example opposite and find out how to recognise genre features in a text and appreciate the way they are being used.

3. Work in groups. Each group should study one of the following sections of the text on page 128.
   a. lines 6–11
   b. lines 12–19
   c. lines 20–25

   Read the text on pages 128–129 again. Then work out how the writer has made the genre features in your section interesting. Report your findings to the rest of the class.

Check! Shut your books and draw a flow chart on a piece of paper showing how you work out what genre a text belongs to and how the writer goes about making the features of the genre interesting.

Step 1 Think about the whole text. What ingredients does it have?
It includes stormy weather, night time, a scientist at work in a laboratory, an experiment, a lifeless being given life.

Step 2 To what genre do these features belong?
- Scientists, laboratories, experiments = science fiction.
- Stormy – night time – monster coming to life = horror.

It was on a dreary night of November that I beheld the accomplishment of my toils. With an anxiety that almost amounted to agony, I collected the instruments of life around me, that I might infuse a spark of being into the lifeless thing that lay at my feet. It was already one in the morning; the rain pattered dismally against the panes, and my candle was nearly burnt out, when, by the glimmer of the half-extinguished light, I saw the dull yellow eye of the creature open; it breathed hard, and convulsive motion agitated its limbs.

Step 3 Look at each part of the text. How has the writer made these genre features interesting?
- By the choice of setting – late at night, with a storm outside.
- By the choice of words, which create the atmosphere, e.g. dreary, anxiety, agony.
- By making the narrator a scientist – this makes it more believable.
- By showing the scientist's strong feelings about what he is doing – this adds to the suspense.
- By building tension through the use of complex sentences.

> C16: Practice

The extract below is taken from a novel called *Frankenstein*, which was written in the nineteenth century by Mary Shelley.

A Victorian scientist called Frankenstein has been working for two years in his laboratory on an experiment. He has been making the body of a human being. Now he hopes to bring the body to life.

Frankenstein

It was on a dreary night of November that I beheld the accomplishment of my toils. With an anxiety that almost amounted to agony, I collected the instruments of life around me, that I might infuse a spark of being into the lifeless thing that lay at my feet. It was already one in the morning; the rain pattered dismally against the panes, and my candle was nearly burnt out, when, by the glimmer of the half-extinguished light,
5 I saw the dull yellow eye of the creature open; it breathed hard, and convulsive motion agitated its limbs.

How can I describe my emotions at this catastrophe, or how delineate the wretch whom with such infinite pains and care I had endeavoured to form? His limbs were in proportion, and I had selected his features as beautiful. Beautiful! – Great God! His yellow skin scarcely covered the work of muscles and arteries beneath; his hair was of a lustrous black, and flowing; his teeth of a pearly whiteness; but these
10 luxuriances only formed a more horrid contrast with his watery eyes, that seemed almost of the same colour as the **dun**-white sockets in which they were set, his shrivelled complexion and straight black lips.

The different accidents of life are not so changeable as the feelings of human nature. I had worked hard for nearly two years, for the sole purpose of infusing life into an inanimate body. For this I had deprived myself of rest and health. I had desired it with an ardour that far exceeded moderation; but now that I had finished, the
15 beauty of the dream vanished, and breathless horror and disgust filled my heart. Unable to endure the aspect of the being I had created, I rushed out of the room, and continued a long time traversing my bedchamber, unable to compose my mind to sleep. At length **lassitude** succeeded the tumult I had before endured; and I threw myself on the bed in my clothes, endeavouring to seek a few moments of forgetfulness. But it was in vain: I slept, indeed, but I was disturbed by the wildest dreams. I thought I saw Elizabeth, in the bloom of health,
20 walking in the streets of Ingolstadt. Delighted and surprised, I embraced her; but as I imprinted the first kiss on her lips, they became **livid** with the **hue** of death; her features appeared to change, and I thought that I held the corpse of my dead mother in my arms; a shroud enveloped her form, and I saw the grave-worms crawling in the folds of the flannel. I started from my sleep with horror; a cold dew covered my forehead, my teeth chattered, and every limb became convulsed: when, by the dim and yellow light of the moon, as it forced its
25 way through the window shutters, I beheld the wretch – the miserable monster whom I had created. He held

up the curtain of the bed; and his eyes, if eyes they may be called, were fixed on me. His jaws opened, and he muttered some inarticulate sounds, while a grin wrinkled his cheeks. He might have spoken, but I did not hear; one hand was stretched out, seemingly to detain me, but I escaped, and rushed downstairs. I took refuge in the courtyard belonging to the house which I inhabited; where I remained during the rest of the night,
30 walking up and down in the greatest agitation, listening attentively, catching and fearing each sound as if it were to announce the approach of the demoniacal corpse to which I had so miserably given life.

> From *Frankenstein* by Mary Shelley

Word bank

dun – dull
lassitude – tiredness
livid – a bluish colour
hue – tint, colour

Questions

1. What does the monster's face look like? Record your answers in a chart like the one below.

Feature	Appearance
Face	
Eyes	
Hair	
Skin	
Teeth	
Lips	

(3 marks)

2. How does the writer feel about the monster in paragraph 2? How can you tell?
(2 marks)

3. The writer has used a series of longer sentences in paragraph 3. How does this choice of sentence structure add to the impact of the description? *(2 marks)*

4. In the first paragraph, how does the writer's use of language to describe the weather and time of day add to the impact of the text? *(3 marks)*

5. How effective is this extract as the opening to a chapter in a horror story?
You should write about:
- the ingredients readers might expect to find
- what happens during this part of the story
- how the monster is described
- how the narrator reacts to the monster coming to life
- the setting
- the writer's use of language. *(5 marks)*

PRACTICE
C17 Sounds amazing

In this unit you will practise responding to the way a playwright reveals the culture of a particular period.

KEY POINTS

Investigating the culture revealed in a text

1. a Read the text on pages 132–133. How can you tell these people are not from the twenty-first century?

   b How does the way someone speaks show what culture they belong to?
   Think about accent, choice of topic, etc.

In the test you may be asked about what a text reveals about the culture it describes. The play from which the extract opposite is taken was first performed in 1914 when people were very aware of belonging to different social classes – working class, middle class, and upper class. It looks at what made someone a member of one class rather than another, and how easy it was to move between classes.

In the extract, two of the characters always speak in standard English and use a sophisticated vocabulary, whereas the third uses much simpler words and occasionally uses slang. This helps to emphasise the difference between the characters and fits in with one of the themes of the play – how the way you speak influences how others see you.

2. Read the example opposite and find out how to investigate what a writer shows readers about the culture in which a text is set.

3. Work in pairs. Read the text on pages 132–133 and note what other differences there are between working-class people (such as the 'upstarts' and the Flower Girl) and middle-class people such as Professor Higgins (the Note Taker). Complete a chart like the one below.

   Hint: What do you discover about their different jobs, lifestyle, education, etc?

4. Work on your own. Look at Colonel Pickering's speeches (the Gentleman) in the text on pages 132–133. To which class does he belong? How can you tell?

Middle-class people	Working-class people
Do jobs like teaching ...	
Are well educated (professor) ...	
Do jobs like ...	
	Aren't as well educated ...

Check! Make a list of four clues you can look for to find out about what a text shows about the culture in which it is set.

Step 1 What is the biggest source of contrast in this part of the text?
The difference between Professor Higgins (the Note Taker) and the way he talks and behaves and the Flower Girl and the way she talks and behaves.

Step 2 How has the writer emphasised the differences between Higgins and the Flower Girl?
Look for these clues in the text:
- Names
  'Note Taker/Professor Higgins' – this emphasises that he is educated. 'The Flower Girl' suggests that it doesn't matter what her name is, that she doesn't have a name, just a job – it's as if she isn't an individual.
- What people do
  Professor Higgins writes and makes notes. The Flower Girl cries and moans.
  Professor Higgins earns money teaching people how to speak differently. The Flower Girl earns her money selling flowers.
- What people talk about
  Higgins says it's a time when people are trying to move up the social ladder. He tells the girl off for speaking so badly.
- How people speak
  Professor Higgins always uses standard English; the Flower Girl is the only person to use non-standard English – 'Garn' – which is slang.

Step 3 What does this text suggest about the culture?
In this culture the way people speak, how educated they are and what kinds of jobs they do are important. It divides them into classes.

The Note Taker This is an age of upstarts. Men begin in Kentish Town with £80 a year, and end in Park Lane with a hundred thousand. They want to drop Kentish Town; but they give themselves away every time they open their mouths. Now I can teach them –

The Flower Girl Let him mind his own business and leave a poor girl –

The Note Taker (*explosively*) Woman: cease this detestable boohooing instantly; or else seek the shelter of some other place of worship.

The Flower Girl (*with feeble defiance*) I've a right to be here if I like, same as you.

The Note Taker A woman who utters such depressing and disgusting sounds has no right to be anywhere – no right to live. Remember that you are a human being with a soul and the divine gift of articulate speech: that your native language is the language of Shakespeare and Milton and The Bible; and don't sit there crooning like a bilious pigeon.

The Flower Girl (*quite overwhelmed, looking up at him in mingled wonder and deprecation without daring to raise her head*) Ah-ah-ah-ow-ow-ow-oo!

> C17: Practice

Below is an extract from George Bernard Shaw's play *Pygmalion*, which was first performed in 1914. In this extract Professor Higgins (the Note Taker) shows his companions that he can tell which part of London a flower seller comes from, just by hearing her speak.

The Gentleman	(*returning to his former place on the note taker's left*) How do you do it, if I may ask?
The Note Taker	Simply phonetics. The science of speech. That's my profession: also my hobby. Happy is the man who can make a living by his hobby! You can spot an Irishman or a Yorkshireman by his **brogue**. *I can place any man within six miles. I can place him within two miles in London. Sometimes within two streets.*
The Flower Girl	Ought to be ashamed of himself, unmanly coward!
The Gentleman	But is there a living in that?

(line 5 marked)

10	**The Note Taker**	Oh, yes. Quite a fat one. This is an age of upstarts. Men begin in Kentish Town with £80 a year, and end in Park Lane with a hundred thousand. They want to drop Kentish Town; but they give themselves away every time they open their mouths. Now I can teach them –
15	**The Flower Girl**	Let him mind his own business and leave a poor girl –
	The Note Taker	(*explosively*) Woman: cease this detestable boohooing instantly; or else seek the shelter of some other place of worship.
	The Flower Girl	(*with feeble defiance*) I've a right to be here if I like, same as you.
20	**The Note Taker**	A woman who utters such depressing and disgusting sounds has no right to be anywhere – no right to live. Remember that you are a human being with a soul and the divine gift of **articulate** speech: that your native language is the language of Shakespeare and Milton and The Bible; and don't sit there crooning like a **bilious** pigeon.
25	**The Flower Girl**	(*quite overwhelmed, looking up at him in mingled wonder and* **deprecation** *without daring to raise her head*) Ah-ah-ah-ow-ow-ow-oo!
	The Note Taker	(*whipping out his book*) Heavens! what a sound! (*He writes; then holds out the book and reads, reproducing her vowels exactly*) Ah-ah-ah-ow-ow-ow-oo!
	The Flower Girl	(*tickled by the performance, and laughing in spite of herself*) Garn!
30	**The Note Taker**	You see this creature with her kerbstone English: the English that will keep her in the gutter to the end of her days. Well, sir, in three months I could pass that girl off as a duchess at an ambassador's garden party. I could even get her a place as lady's maid or shop assistant, which requires better English.
35	**The Flower Girl**	What's that you say?
	The Note Taker	Yes, you squashed cabbage leaf, you disgrace to the noble architecture of these columns, you incarnate insult to the English language: I could pass you off as the Queen of Sheba. (*To the Gentleman*) Can you believe that?
40	**The Gentleman**	Of course I can. I am myself a student of Indian dialects; and–
	The Note Taker	(*eagerly*) Are you? Do you know Colonel Pickering, the author of Spoken Sanscrit?
	The Gentleman	I am Colonel Pickering. Who are you?
	The Note Taker	Henry Higgins, author of Higgins's Universal Alphabet.
45	**Pickering**	(*with enthusiasm*) I came from India to meet you.
	Higgins	I was going to India to meet you.
	Pickering	Where do you live?
	Higgins	27A Wimpole Street. Come and see me tomorrow.
50	**Pickering**	I'm at the Carlton. Come with me now and let's have a jaw over some supper.

> From *Pygmalion* by George Bernard Shaw

Word bank

brogue – a strong accent
articulate – able to speak clearly and fluently
bilious – bad-tempered
deprecation – disapproval

> C17: Practice

↘ Questions

1. What books have Colonel Pickering and Professor Higgins written? *(1 mark)*

2. a Read lines 10–14. Why do people want Professor Higgins to teach them to speak differently? *(1 mark)*

   b Read lines 30–34. What does Professor Higgins suggest he believes is the only difference between a flower girl or a shop assistant and a duchess? *(1 mark)*

3. The writer uses a dash in two different ways in the text. Can you explain what it is used for in:
   a line 15 ('leave a poor girl –')?
   b line 20 ('– no right to live')? *(2 marks)*

4. How does the order of the clauses in the following sentence help to make Professor Higgins's comment more amusing?

   > Remember that you are a human being with a soul and the divine gift of articulate speech: that your native language is the language of Shakespeare and Milton and The Bible; and don't sit there crooning like a bilious pigeon. (lines 20–23)

   (2 marks)

5. How has the writer emphasised the difference in social class between the Flower Girl and Professor Higgins?
   You should write about:
   - their jobs
   - the way they speak
   - what they say to each other
   - how Colonel Pickering responds to each of them. *(5 marks)*

PRACTICE
C18 Whose face is it, anyway?

In this unit you will practise investigating how writers create a relationship with their readers through the way they structure their texts.

KEY POINTS

Appreciating the relationship a writer creates with the audience

1. Read the text on pages 137–138. Then study the six key features of a text, listed below. Talk about how each feature could be used to show a writer's train of thought.

   The six key features of a text to study when you look at its structure are:
   - title
   - introduction
   - conclusion
   - topic sentences
   - link words
   - connectives.

   In the test you may be asked to write about the relationship a writer has created with readers. The text on pages 137–138 is a newspaper column written for the *Daily Telegraph* by Professor Steve Jones. The column is called 'View from the lab' and Steve Jones is an expert writing about technical topics for a non-expert readership. His purpose is to entertain and inform his readers while making sure that they will want to read his column again. This means that his texts have to be clear and easy to follow, even when they are explaining quite complex topics, and he has to create a relationship with his readers. He does this by creating the right tone and presenting himself as a likeable person.

2. Read the example on page 136 and find out how to spot the way the writer has:
   a. made the text clear and easy to follow
   b. built a relationship with the audience.

3. Work in teams. Read the text on pages 137–138. Which team can find:
   a. the six key features and explain how each makes the text clear?
   b. the most examples of the writer revealing his own personality?

Check! Close your books. First list six key features that are used to organise a text. Then explain how a writer can create a relationship with the audience.

> C18: Practice

Step 1 How has the writer made the organisation of the text clear?
Find and study any key features that are used in the part of the text you are reading.
- Topic sentence – used to introduce readers to the Timewatch programme and Steve Jones's part in it.

Step 2 How has the writer created a relationship with the audience?
Look for the following.
- Personal information that the reader can identify with.
- The picture the writer creates of himself.

- Questions that set readers wondering or agreeing with the writer's view.
- Brackets that are used to add in the writer's comments.
- Parts of the text where the writer comes across as chatty and informal placed next to parts where the text is more formal or sophisticated.

Last week I played a minor part in an otherwise interesting BBC Timewatch on grammar school boys. It had pictures of 'then' versus 'now' (not, in my case, a flattering comparison). The producers, as they do, sent out a card to announce the date of the show. It was a reduced version of one of those vast group photographs, with pupils in their hundreds, teachers in the favourable ratio of those days, and gowns, blazers, ties and the glum faces of the Fifties in abundance.

Ah, what memories! I could easily spot my class at Wirral Grammar School, the flower of Liverpool's Left Bank. There they all were, Anyon, Backhouse, Baker, Beck, Bunn; neatly lined up in order, to Williams via a 12-year-old Jones. What, I wonder, became of them?

But then, a nasty surprise. The older boys were wearing striped jackets, which we did not. A second look showed that it was not Wirral Grammar at all but another (and, from the stripes, rather snottier) institution. Art had imitated nature and I was fooled into seeing people who were not there.

136

Below is a newspaper article written by Professor Steve Jones, in which he explains why it is sometimes difficult to recognise people's faces.

View from the lab: Let's face it, the eye can play strange tricks

By Professor Steve Jones

PAINTING, according to John Constable, is a science, 'a branch of natural philosophy, of which pictures are but experiments'.

At the Scottish National Portrait Gallery in Edinburgh is a new exhibition, **The Science of the Face**, with a marvellous book, **In the Eye of the Beholder**, to go with it.

Why are we so keen on portraits and so good at telling faces apart? Two scrunched-up newspapers (even copies of the Guardian and the Daily Telegraph) look much the same, although their shapes are quite different, while two faces are distinct although their shapes are almost the same. There is something wired into our brains that is so sensitive that it can recognise people with amazing accuracy.

At least, it ought to. Last week I played a minor part in an otherwise interesting BBC Timewatch on grammar school boys. It had pictures of 'then' versus 'now' (not, in my case, a flattering comparison). The producers, as they do, sent out a card to announce the date of the show. It was a reduced version of one of those vast group photographs, with pupils in their hundreds, teachers in the favourable ratio of those days, and gowns, blazers, ties and the glum faces of the Fifties in abundance.

Ah, what memories! I could easily spot my class at Wirral Grammar School, the flower of Liverpool's Left Bank. There they all were, Anyon, Backhouse, Baker, Beck, Bunn; neatly lined up in order, to Williams via a 12-year-old Jones. What, I wonder, became of them?

But then, a nasty surprise. The

older boys were wearing striped jackets, which we did not. A second look showed that it was not Wirral Grammar at all but another (and, from the stripes, rather snottier) institution. Art had imitated nature and I was fooled into seeing people who were not there.

And that's where the science – and the exhibition – comes in. To recognise a face is not a simple thing. As artists have long known (Salvador Dali often made the point) it depends on scale, on position and on context. One of the more alarming portraits on display turns from Blair into Thatcher as the viewer steps away from it: Tony is in the details, but Maggie makes the big picture.

A simple bar code contains most of the information in the face. It consists of six stripes – hair, forehead, eyebrows, nose, lips and chin. The school photograph was just too small to contain it. A full-face picture, such as a school photo, is also harder to identify than one seen slightly from the side, because the latter contains three-dimensional information (the shape of the nose, a furtive ear) that the other has lost.

Some people are bad at faces. They use clues from voice, clothes or place to tell people apart. **In the Eye of the Beholder** describes how one such individual was engaged in a lawsuit. Wandering into court, he discussed his case with a barrister – but the wrong one: not his own, but his opponent's. After all, the context was right; a lawyer, with a gown, in a courtroom. Only the face did not fit. Needless to say, he lost. I, too, assumed that a school photograph must be of my own school; and so strong was that idea that it led to false perception.

The law once put great faith in 'photofits', pictures composed of cut-up mouths, noses and eyes. They do not work, because, like the Timewatch card, they are small, square-on and set firmly in context. The context problem can lead to injustice. If an innocent person on an identity parade looks like a photofit then he may be doomed simply because a picture of someone like him has been seen in a criminal setting – even if he looks nothing like the real villain.

The study of faces brings the arts and the sciences close together. So strong is the urge to find them – and a baby will respond to one within minutes of birth – that we see a human face on the moon. Foolish people have persuaded themselves that there is another visage in the Viking photograph of a mountain-range on Mars; proof, of course, of an extinct race trying to send us a mute message. NASA has recently published better images from the planet, and now the mountains just look like mountains. No doubt, the credulous will continue to believe in Martians. If they were mugged by the Man in the Moon would they pick him out in an identity parade?

> From the *Daily Telegraph*, 23rd April 1998

⬇ Questions

1. What information are readers given about Steve Jones's time at school? *(2 marks)*

2. What does Steve Jones suggest about his part in the TV programme when he says:

   > Last week I played a minor part in an otherwise interesting BBC Timewatch on grammar school boys. (lines 22–25)

   (2 marks)

3. a. How does the writer's use of different types of sentences in paragraph 6 help to show readers how surprised he was? *(2 marks)*

   b. The writer uses brackets in lines 12–14, 26–27, 48–49 and 56–57. What impact do they have in each case? *(4 marks)*

4. Read lines 44–63. What effect does using different types of vocabulary have on the impression Steve Jones creates of himself? *(2 marks)*

5. How has Steve Jones made sure that readers will be convinced by his argument that faces are harder to recognise than we think?
   You should write about:
   - the way the whole text is organised
   - the way paragraphs are structured
   - the writer's choice of examples
   - the variety of sentence structures used
   - the tone the writer creates. *(5 marks)*

⬇ Comparing texts

Read carefully the extract from *Frankenstein* on pages 128–129, the extract from *Pygmalion* on pages 132–133 and 'View from the lab' on pages 137–138. All the writers set out to entertain their readers. Explain three differences in the way the writers do this.

(3 marks)

D Preparing for the Key Stage 3 reading test

Introduction

At the end of Year 9 you will take the Key Stage 3 National Curriculum English tests. There are three test papers: reading, writing and Shakespeare. These tests will help you and your teacher to see how much progress you have made since you took the Key Stage 2 English test at the end of Year 6. You may have measured your progress in the optional tests for Year 7 and Year 8, and you will find that the Year 9 tests are similar in many ways.

So far this book has focused on the skills you need to improve your reading and has provided plenty of practice to help you prepare for the reading test. This section focuses on the test papers themselves and:

- explains what is involved in the reading test
- provides practice tests so that you become more familiar with the kinds of texts and questions that you will meet in the tests.

The reading paper

The reading paper lasts for 75 minutes, which includes 15 minutes to read the texts before you are allowed to look at the questions. In the test you will be given a reading booklet that contains the texts and an answer booklet in which to write your answers.

The texts

You will be asked to read three texts from a variety of different text types, such as:
- an extract from a novel or short story
- an information text
- a piece of literary non-fiction, such as travel writing.

The texts will be linked by a theme or common subject, such as the natural world or sport. The link between the three texts is explained in the reading booklet to make sure that you understand what sort of text you are reading, especially if it is an extract.

The reading time

You should use the 15 minutes of reading time at the beginning of the test to:
- get an overall idea of what the texts are about
- think about the *text type*, and what that means, for example, how much use of imagery or unusual vocabulary is there in a literary text?
- think about the writer's purpose in writing the text
- consider the effect the text has on you and what causes that effect, for example, the style of writing could make you laugh or the subject matter could be about a topic that is completely new to you

- identify any striking or original uses of language
- note anything that you find difficult to understand so that you can return to it later.

The questions

The reading paper will contain different types of questions to test your reading skills, and will focus on five key areas:

1. identifying information or ideas and quoting from the text when required.
2. working out meanings that are implicit. This means that you will have to 'read between the lines' of the text to work out what is meant.
3. explaining the structure and organisation of a text, for example, how different parts relate to each other or how the writer has used grammar and different kinds of sentences to create meaning.
4. commenting on the writer's choice and use of language.
5. explaining the writer's purpose and the overall meaning and effect of a text, and how it affects you as a reader.

The different types of questions that test these skills include:

- Questions that carry only one mark and require short answers. This type of question may ask you to complete a table or copy a word or phrase from the text to show that you have understood its meaning.
- Questions worth two, three or four marks. For these questions you may be asked to find several pieces of information in the text or write a couple of sentences explaining something about the text.
- Questions worth five marks. These require the longest answers and will sometimes have a series of bullet-pointed 'prompts' to help you to structure your answer and decide what to include in it.

The number of marks given to a question and the space allowed in the answer booklet for writing your answer will give you a clue as to how detailed your answer should be and how much time you should spend on a question.

Giving the best answers to the questions

In order to get full marks it is important that you:

- **do exactly what you are asked**. For example, if you are told to copy something from the text, you will get no marks if you put it into your own words
- **answer the question that is asked**. Make sure that you include only material that answers the question. Including any other material will waste your time and waste space in your answer booklet
- **use textual detail whenever you are told to do so**. Make sure that you use direct quotations if you are commenting on language use or grammar
- **respond to *all* the prompts** (such as bullet points), if any are given
- **complete all the questions in the time allowed**. Plan your time carefully, but if you run out of time, make sure you attempt as many questions with high marks as you can.

> **Preparing for the Key Stage 3 reading test**

Marks

The reading paper is worth 32 marks overall. These marks are divided between the five key reading skills explained on page 141.

Express yourself well

Here are a few tips for writing good answers.
- Write in **full sentences**, unless the question states otherwise. In a test your style should be formal.
- Think about your **handwriting** even if you are in a hurry. After all, you cannot score marks if the marker cannot read what you have written!
- For the longer answers, take time to **plan your answer**. Read the question carefully, make notes and plan what you are going to say. At the end of planning your answer, check that you have actually answered the question and that you are not going to write about things for which you were not asked.
- Watch your **spelling** and think about **punctuation**. Do not make your sentences too long. Take care to use apostrophes, quotation marks and commas correctly.
- Make sure that what you have written **makes sense**. If, as you read through what you have written, you realise it does not make sense, change it. If you cannot understand what you have written, it is unlikely that the marker will.
- Try to leave a few minutes at the end to **check your answers** carefully.

Using the practice tests

There are two practice reading tests in this section, which follow the format, length and timing of the actual test. If you attempt these tests during Year 9, the results will show you and your teacher where you have improved your reading skills since Year 8. The results will also highlight areas of your reading skills that might still be improved before you take the actual test. You can then go back through this book and revise the skills and strategies you need.

Your teacher will give you copies of the reading booklets and the answer booklets, which contain lines for you to write your answers. You can then practise the tests exactly as they appear in the actual Key Stage 3 tests.

Your teacher will mark the practice tests and give you a total score for each test. He or she will also be able to tell you a National Curriculum level to which the score corresponds.

When you receive the results of the actual Key Stage 3 tests, the marks for both the reading paper and the Shakespeare reading task will be combined to give you an overall National Curriculum level for reading. You will also receive a separate National Curriculum level for writing, and a combined reading and writing level for English. This will show you exactly what your strengths and weaknesses are, and will allow you to focus on areas that will improve your reading skills beyond Key Stage 3.

Good luck!

Reading test 1
Against the Odds

Remember

- The test is 1 hour 15 minutes long.
- You have 15 minutes to read the following texts before answering the questions on pages 147–151. During this time you should not look at the questions.
- You then have 1 hour to write your answers.
- There are 14 questions totalling 32 marks on this paper.
- The spaces for answers and the number of marks indicate how much you need to write.

Contents

On Trial   page 144
A Pang of Regret   page 145
Lillian Board   page 146

Introduction

For many people, playing or watching sport is an important part of their lives. Many memorable moments may be linked with sporting occasions or sports personalities. The lives of top-level sportspeople are a source of great interest, and as much is often written about them as about their sporting achievements.

Tony Adams, the former Arsenal and England footballer, recalls an incident in his early teens that had an important effect on his future attitude towards the sport. This is an extract from his autobiography, *Addicted*.

On Trial

By now it was becoming clear that I had a chance of making it as a professional footballer, which was all I wanted. Everyone was telling me I was good and, to be honest, I knew I was. Before the football really kicked in, I had always felt inadequate and a loner; I could be lonely in a crowd. I had never been able to resist the mass kickabouts in the park, though, even if it took some courage for me to ask to play. I don't know why, because I did know that once the game started, everyone would respect me and would want this shy timid kid on their side. Once I was in a football environment, I was the main man. Later on, 'equal' sides consisted of me picking three players against 20 on the other team, though even then sometimes I was told to go in goal because they thought I was too good in the outfield.

I remember in my early teens praying to be a professional, just wishing really, but it was to stand me in good stead, even if in those days my idea of a God was a warped one of a figure who could just make my dreams come true. That emerged from an incident that probably spurred me on in my early career more than anything.

At the age of 13 I had made it into the last 30 for the following season's England Under-15 Schoolboys side and there was to be a trial at Lilleshall National Sports Centre in Shropshire to decide on the last 22. The day before, the eight London boys selected travelled up together on the train from Euston. That night I remember praying to be in the England team.

I had this strange feeling about the trial match that took place. At previous trials, all the people in charge had been so friendly towards me. Now there was a strange, frosty atmosphere. Nobody spoke to me. I was handed a No. 13 shirt and was told to stand behind the goal, out of the way. It was the same for five other London boys. We were discarded. They had found an easy way to whittle the squad down.

We were told that we had been seen misbehaving on the train journey the previous day by an education officer travelling independently and who had reported us. There had been some minor, high-spirited scuffling among a few of the lads, which involved some coffee being thrown and a bit of bad language by one or two.

I had certainly not been a part of any of it, though. I was sitting in the corner, trying to mind my own business, but because I stood out as tall for my age, I was one of those pointed out. It all felt so unjust and left me fuming. God had not answered my prayer. The rejection – a feeling which I would come to recognise as a huge motivating force in my life – was intensely painful to me at that age. 'Right,' I remember saying to myself then. 'I'm going to do it my way from now on.' I was going to redouble my efforts to become a pro.

> **Reading test 1**

In this extract from L. P. Hartley's novel *The Go-Between*, Leo (the young narrator of the story) describes the end of a cricket match. The teams represent the family who live at Brandham Hall, a large country house in Norfolk where Leo is staying as a guest, and the villagers. Lord Trimingham is captain of the Hall team. Ted is the local blacksmith and star batsman for the village team. The story is set in 1900.

A Pang of Regret

I could not tell whether the next ball was on the wicket or not, but it was pitched much further up and suddenly I saw Ted's face and body swinging round, and the ball, travelling towards me on a rising straight line like a cable stretched between us. Ted started to run and then stopped and stood watching me, wonder in his eyes and a wild disbelief.

   I threw my hand above my head and the ball stuck there, but the impact knocked me over. When I scrambled up, still clutching the ball to me, as though it was a pain that had started in my heart, I heard the sweet sound of applause and saw the field breaking up and Lord Trimingham coming towards me. I can't remember what he said – my emotions were too overwhelming – but I remember that his congratulations were the more precious because they were reserved and understated, they might, in fact, have been addressed to a *man*; and it was as a man, and not by any means the least of men, that I joined the group who were making their way back to the pavilion. We went together in a ragged cluster, the defeated and the surviving batsmen with us, all enmity laid aside, amid a more than generous measure of applause from the spectators. I could not tell how I felt; in my high mood of elation the usual landmarks by which I judged such things were lost to view. I was still in the air, though the scaffolding of events which had lifted me had crumbled. But I was still aware of one separate element that had not quite fused in the general concourse of passions; the pang of regret, sharp as a sword-thrust, that had accompanied the catch. Far from diminishing my exultation, it had somehow raised it to a higher power, like the drop of bitter in the fount of happiness; but I felt that I should be still happier – that it would add another cubit to my stature – if I told Ted of it. Something warned me that such an avowal would be unorthodox; the personal feelings of cricketers were concealed behind their stiff upper lips. But I was almost literally above myself; I knew that the fate of the match had turned on me, and I felt I could afford to defy convention. Yet how would he take it? What were his feelings? Was he still elated by his innings or was he bitterly disappointed by its untimely close? Did he still regard me as a friend, or as an enemy who had brought about his downfall? I did not greatly care; and seeing that he was walking alone (most of the players had exhausted their stock of conversation) I sidled up to him and said, 'I'm sorry Ted. I didn't really mean to catch you out.' He stopped and smiled at me. 'Well, that's very handsome of you,' he said. 'It was a damned good catch, anyway. I never thought you'd hold it. To tell you the truth I'd forgotten all about you being at square leg, and then I looked round and there you were, by God. And then I thought, "It'll go right over his head," but you stretched up like a concertina. I'd thought of a dozen ways I might get out, but never thought I'd be caught out by you.' 'I didn't mean to,' I repeated, not to be cheated of my apology. At that moment the clapping grew louder and some enthusiasts coupled Ted's name with it. Though we were all heroes, he was evidently the crowd's favourite; and I dropped back so that he might walk in alone.

> Reading test 1

This is an obituary of the athlete Lillian Board, which appeared in the *Daily Telegraph* shortly after her death. Lillian Board was one of the best-known athletes of her time – one of the first sports superstars in many ways – and there was a great feeling of shock that she should die at such a young age and with such a bright future ahead of her.

Lillian Board

LILLIAN BOARD, who died in a Munich hospital, combined a rare athletic brilliance at every event from 100 to 800 metres with beauty and a vivacious personality. She was just 22. That she had only just started to nibble at the honours she would inevitably have gained was demonstrated by the manner in which she won two European gold medals in 1969 with limited training after injury. In a three-year spell she finished fifth in the 1966 Commonwealth Games 440 yards, won the women's AAA title in 1967, the Olympic silver medal for the 400 metres in 1968, and finally the 800 metres and 4×400 metres in the European Championships in Athens.

Miss Board and her twin sister Irene were born in Durban and returned with their Manchester-born parents to live in West London in 1950. At $14\frac{1}{2}$ she had already made her mark by winning the English Schools junior long jump, and her coaching was taken in hand by her father George, who dedicated his spare time to supervising her athletics, attending every training session in fair weather or foul.

When she was only $17\frac{1}{2}$ the dividends from the endless hours of hard work and perseverance paid off. She was selected to run in the Commonwealth Games in Jamaica and did better than expected. The following year she defeated Judy Pollock, the world record holder, in Los Angeles during the United States v Commonwealth match in 52.8 sec, a second faster than she had run before.

After a brilliant season in 1968 she went to Mexico as favourite for the Olympic 400 metres and confirmed the rating with two good preliminary runs. In the final, however, after a nervous start and a too-fast first half she was pipped by the French girl Colette Besson by a mere $\frac{7}{100}$ ths of a second. She gained ample revenge in Athens with an enthralling last leg in the 4×400 metres. This was possibly her greatest run, for by then she was an 800 metres specialist and had scarcely prepared for the 400 metres. Even though she had won the 800 metres with a surprising facility she was by no means at her fittest as a result of a combination of a persistent back strain and an early-season dental operation.

During the early part of the 1970 summer it was obvious things were not quite right for she was in pain whenever she trained. By mid-June her ability to complete the season was in doubt. She ran her last race on June 20, finishing third in the 800 metres at the women's championships. On June 29 she said she would have to withdraw from England's Commonwealth Games team. Shortly afterwards she entered hospital, which she left on October 23. Her desperate last hope flight to Munich came on November 7.

Her loss is a more than usually tragic one. She had started to show flair as a dress designer and her future seemed assured. As charming off the track as she was single-minded in the pursuit of victory on it, she never let us forget that she loved to be considered part of the swinging Seventies, mini-skirts and all – not just an athletic freak. The sporting world will mourn her.

Reading test 1
Against the Odds

> **Questions 1–5 are about *On Trial* (on page 144).**

1. In paragraph 1, why is the word 'equal' in inverted commas?

   _____

   _____

   (1 mark)

2. Explain how the writer structures the first paragraph. You should comment on:

   - the connectives;
   - the verb forms;
   - the subject matter.

   - _____

     _____

   - _____

     _____

   - _____

     _____

   (3 marks)

3. From paragraph 2, and using your own words, explain what the writer now feels about his childhood concept of God.

   _____

   _____

   (1 mark)

4. From paragraph 5, find and copy two words or phrases which convey the writer's attitude about what happened on the train. Explain what attitude these words convey.

   (2 marks)

	Attitude conveyed
Word/phrase 1	
Word/phrase 2	

5. From the extract as a whole, what sort of person does the writer seem to be? You should comment on:
   - his character or personality, and how it has changed;
   - what other people think of him.

   _____

(5 marks)

Questions 6–9 are about *A Pang of Regret* (on page 145).

6. a) In the first paragraph, what is the effect of the simile 'like a cable stretched between us'?

   _____

(1 mark)

   b) Find and copy two other similes used in the extract.

   • _____
   • _____

(1 mark)

7. In your own words, explain why Leo particularly enjoys Lord Trimingham's congratulations.

   _____

   _____

   (1 mark)

8. What makes it possible for Leo to approach Ted and apologise to him?

   _____

   _____

   _____

   (2 marks)

9. Describe Leo's feelings and the reasons for them after he caught the ball.
   You should comment on:
   - how he feels about himself;
   - how he feels about Ted;
   - how he thinks he ought to behave in this situation.

   _____

   _____

   _____

   _____

   _____

   _____

   _____

   _____

   _____

   _____

   _____

   _____

   _____

   _____

   _____

   _____

   (5 marks)

> Reading test 1

Questions 10–13 are about *Lillian Board* (on page 146).

10. How soon after winning the English Schools junior long jump competition was Lillian Board selected to run in the Commonwealth Games in Jamaica?

   _____

   (1 mark)

11. Explain the meaning and effect of each of these words: *nibbled* (paragraph 1) and *pipped* (paragraph 4).

   - _____
     _____

   - _____
     _____

   (2 marks)

12. a) In paragraph 4, what two connectives does the writer use to signal a shift in tone from the opening sentence?

   - _____   • _____

   (1 mark)

   b) How do these connectives change the tone in this paragraph?

   _____
   _____

   (1 mark)

13. What does the writer suggest about Lillian Board in the last sentence of paragraph 6?

   _____
   _____
   _____

   (2 marks)

> Reading test 1

Question 14 is about *On Trial* and *Lillian Board* (pages 144 and 146)

14. Both *On Trial* and *Lillian Board* are non-fiction texts. As well as similarities, there are some differences between them. Comment on three features of these texts which are different.

(3 marks)

Feature	*On Trial*	*Lillian Board*
1		
2		
3		

Reading test 2
In a Fog!

Remember

- The test is 1 hour 15 minutes long.
- You have 15 minutes to read the following texts before answering the questions on pages 157–160. During this time you should not look at the questions.
- You then have 1 hour to write your answers.
- There are 14 questions totalling 32 marks on this paper.
- The spaces for answers and the number of marks indicate how much you need to write.

Contents

Fog Everywhere   page 153
Nature's Fog Machine   page 154
The Great Smog of 1952   pages 155–156

Introduction

The weather often affects the way we live and how we feel about our lives. Although we cannot control the weather, it is becoming increasingly clear that the way we treat our environment can influence the climate generally, and may seriously affect specific weather conditions.

This is an extract from the opening chapter of *Bleak House* by Charles Dickens. The plot of the novel revolves around a long-running and complicated legal case. Although the fog that Dickens describes feels very real, he uses it as a metaphor for the confusion and murkiness that lie at the heart of his story.

Fog Everywhere

Fog everywhere. Fog up the river, where it flows among green aits and meadows; fog down the river, where it rolls defiled among the tiers of shipping and the waterside pollutions of a great (and dirty) city. Fog on the Essex marshes, fog on the Kentish heights. Fog creeping into the cabooses of collier-brigs; fog lying out on the yards and hovering in the rigging of great ships; fog drooping on the gunwales of barges and small boats. Fog in the eyes and throats of ancient Greenwich pensioners, wheezing by the firesides of their wards; fog in the stem and bowl of the afternoon pipe of the wrathful skipper, down in his close cabin; fog cruelly pinching the toes and fingers of his shivering little 'prentice boy on deck. Chance people on the bridges peeping over the parapets into a nether sky of fog, with fog all round them, as if they were up in a balloon and hanging in the misty clouds.

In this extract from *The Rough Guide to the Weather*, Robert Henson explains how fog is formed. He also discusses different kinds of fog which may be caused by different atmospheric or environmental conditions.

NATURE'S FOG MACHINE

As with any other cloud, the trick to **making fog** is to either cool the air so much that some water vapour is effectively squeezed out, or to add so much water vapour that some of it is forced to condense into cloud. Either way, you're left with more moisture than can remain in vapour form at a given temperature. Some of it then gets deposited onto salt, dust, soot and whatever else is lying around. Each of the resulting water-coated particles measures in the region of 10–20 micrometers/400–800 millionths of an inch.

It doesn't take much moisture to make fog. If a batch of fog materialized in an ordinary living room, it might represent only about 3.1 grams, or about one-tenth of an ounce of water. That's barely enough to coat the bottom of a drinking glass. An identical amount of water can produce a thin fog or a pea-souper, depending on whether it's distributed across a small or large number of particles. Back in Victorian England, when unrestricted coal-burning was the rule, there was so much airborne soot for moisture to cling to that the era's 'stinking fogs' were far thicker than they are now.

Fog close to the **ocean** tends to form on **airborne salt**, a process that can happen even when the relative humidity is as low as 70 per cent. The thin obscuration that results – **haze** – can lower visibility to a few miles or kilometres. In cities, the tons of pollution spewed out by cars and factories leads to the urban equivalent of haze: **smog**, a word that conjoins smoke and fog. (Hawaii even has something called vog, a product of water adhering to the ash and other debris emitted by the island's volcanic peaks.)

The lines between haze, smog and fog are rather fuzzy. Water is more attracted to some particles (like salt) than to others. If lots of these water-attracting (hygroscopic) particles are to hand, then fog can form at humidities on the order of 95 per cent rather than the fully saturated 100 per cent. In major urban areas, pollutants alone can restrict views below the fog criterion without the help of moisture. Some dank days are informally tagged as foggy or hazy when they're actually just dirty.

The official website of the United Kingdom Meteorological Office contains much general information about climate and the weather as well as daily weather forecasts. This text gives an account of the worst fog – or rather smog – ever to envelop London.

The Great Smog of 1952

Since Roman times, if not before, Britain has been known to people abroad as a land of mists and fogs. Until recently, indeed, visitors to the capital could take home with them tins of 'London fog'! For hundreds of years, the mists and fogs of Britain's major cities were all too often polluted and noxious, with London especially badly affected. The fogs endangered health and also posed a threat to travellers who lost their way and thus became an easy prey to robbers.

The smoke-laden fog that shrouded the capital from Friday 5 December to Tuesday 9 December 1952 brought premature death to thousands and inconvenience to millions. An estimated 4,000 died because of it. Road, rail and air transport were brought almost to a standstill and a performance at the Sadler's Wells Theatre had to be suspended when fog in the auditorium made conditions intolerable for the audience and performers.

During the day on 5 December, the fog was not especially dense and generally possessed a dry, smoky character. When nightfall came, however, the fog thickened. Visibility dropped to a few metres. The following day, the sun was too low in the sky to make much of an impression on the fog. That night and on the Sunday and Monday nights, the fog again thickened. In many parts of London, it was impossible at night for pedestrians to find their way, even in familiar districts.

In the Isle of Dogs, the visibility was at times nil. The fog there was so thick that people could not see their own feet! Even in the drier thoroughfares of central London, the fog was exceptionally thick. Not until 9 December did it clear. In central London, the visibility remained below 500 metres continuously for 114 hours and below 50 metres continuously for 48 hours. At Heathrow Airport, visibility remained below ten metres for almost 48 hours from the morning of 6 December.

continued overleaf

continued

Huge quantities of impurities were released into the atmosphere during the period in question. On each day during the foggy period, the following amounts of pollutants were emitted: 1,000 tonnes of smoke particles, 2,000 tonnes of carbon dioxide, 140 tonnes of hydrochloric acid and 14 tonnes of fluorine compounds. In addition, and perhaps most dangerously, 370 tonnes of sulphur dioxide were converted into 800 tonnes of sulphuric acid. At London's County Hall, the concentration of smoke in the air increased from 0.49 milligrams per cubic metre on 4 December to 4.46 on the 7th and 8th.

The infamous fog of December 1952 has come to be known as 'The Great Smog'; the term 'smog' being a portmanteau word meaning 'fog intensified by smoke'. The term was coined almost half a century earlier, by H. A. Des Voeux, who first used it in 1905 to describe the conditions of fuliginous (sooty) fog that occurred all too often over British urban areas. It was popularised in 1911 when Des Voeux presented to the Manchester Conference of the Smoke Abatement League of Great Britain a report on the deaths that occurred in Glasgow and Edinburgh in the Autumn of 1909 as a consequence of smoke-laden fogs.

Legislation followed the Great Smog of 1952 in the form of the City of London (Various Powers) Act of 1954 and the Clean Air Acts of 1956 and 1968. These Acts banned emissions of black smoke and decreed that residents of urban areas and operators of factories must convert to smokeless fuels. As these residents and operators were necessarily given time to convert, however, fogs continued to be smoky for some time after the Act of 1956 was passed. In 1962, for example, 750 Londoners died as a result of a fog, but nothing on the scale of the 1952 Great Smog has ever occurred again.

Pea-soupers have become a thing of the past, thanks partly to pollution legislation but also to slum clearance, urban renewal and the widespread use of central heating in the houses and offices of British towns and cities. As recently as the early 1960s, winter sunshine totals were thirty per cent lower in the smokier districts of London than in the rural areas around the capital. Today, there is little difference.

We should not, however, be complacent. The air now contains other types of pollutants, many of them from vehicle exhausts. Among these pollutants are carbon monoxide, nitrogen dioxide, ozone, benzines and aldehydes. They are less visible than the pollutants of yesteryear but are equally toxic, causing eye irritation, asthma and bronchial complaints. To some extent, we have simply replaced one form of air pollution with another. We may question whether or not the major cities of the British Isles are any less polluted now than they have been for hundreds of years.

Reading test 2
In a Fog!

> **Questions 1–4 are about *Fog Everywhere* (on page 153).**

1. Why do you think the writer adds the phrase '(and dirty)' at the end of the second sentence?

   _____
   _____
   _____
   _____

   (2 marks)

2. Comment on the structure and effect of the third sentence: 'Fog on the Essex marshes, fog on the Kentish heights.'

   _____
   _____
   _____

   (1 mark)

3. Find and copy an adverb from the text which conveys the writer's attitude towards the apprentice boy on the ship. Explain what this attitude is.

   Adverb: _____

   Attitude: _____

   (2 marks)

4. What does the writer seem to feel about the fog? You should comment on:
   - what the fog is shown to do;
   - who and what the fog affects;
   - the language used to describe the fog.

   _____
   _____
   _____
   _____
   _____
   _____
   _____
   _____
   _____

_____
_____
_____
_____
_____
_____
_____
_____
_____
_____
_____
_____

(5 marks)

Questions 5–9 are about *Nature's Fog Machine* (on page 154).

5. How many different ways are there to make fog?
   _____
   (1 mark)

6. Haze and pea-souper are two different kinds of fog. Explain how they are different.
   _____
   _____
   (1 mark)

7. Why does haze form so easily close to seas or oceans?
   _____
   _____
   _____
   (2 marks)

8. From paragraph 3, find and copy a verb which shows the writer's attitude towards pollution caused by cars and factories. What attitude does this word convey?

   Verb: _____

   Attitude: _____

   (2 marks)

9. Explain the three different uses of brackets in this text.

(3 marks)

Example	Use
Paragraph 2: (Hawaii ... volcanic peaks)	
Paragraph 3: (like salt)	
Paragraph 3: (hygroscopic)	

Questions 10–13 are about *The Great Smog of 1952* (on pages 155–156).

10. From paragraph 1, give two risks to people caused by fog in the past.

- _____
- _____

(2 marks)

11. Explain why 'shrouded' (paragraph 2) is an effective adjective to describe the smog.

_____
_____

(1 mark)

12. From paragraph 3, identify three ways in which the writer emphasises the unusual conditions which existed during the great smog of 1952. Give examples from the text.

(3 marks)

Way of emphasising unusual conditions	Examples

> Reading test 2

13. What point of view do you think the writer conveys in comparing airborne pollution now with what it was in the past?

    You should comment on:
    - what the writer says has changed;
    - what the writer says has stayed the same;
    - how the writer's choice of language suggest his attitudes or opinions.

    _____
    _____
    _____
    _____
    _____
    _____
    _____
    _____
    _____
    _____
    _____
    _____
    _____
    _____

    (5 marks)

    Question 14 is about *Nature's Fog Machine* (on page 154) and *The Great Smog of 1952* (on pages 155–156).

14. Both *Nature's Fog Machine* and *The Great Smog of 1952* provide the reader with information. However, they do it in ways which are sometimes similar and sometimes different. Identify one similarity and one difference between the texts, and give examples from **both** texts.

    (2 marks)

	Example from *Nature's Fog Machine*	Example from *The Great Smog of 1952*
A similarity between the texts is:		
A difference between the texts is:		

160